A BEGINNERS G

ORGANIZE
Your LIFE

RELAX AND UNWIND WITH AN ORGANIZED HOUSE, LIFE, AND MIND

KRISTEN WILLET

© 2022 A Beginners Guide To Organizing Your Life : Relax and Unwind with an Organized House, Life, and Mind

All rights reserved. No part of the book may be reproduced in any shape or form without permission from the publisher.

This guide is written from a combination of experience and high-level research. Even though we have done our best to ensure this book is accurate and up to date, there are no guarantees to the accuracy or completeness of the contents herein.

ISBN: 9798362640774

REVIEWS

Reviews and feedback help improve this book and the author. If you enjoy this book, we would greatly appreciate it if you could take a few moments to share your opinion and post a review on Amazon.

Download The Audio Version of This Book for Free! If you love listening to audiobooks on-the-go or enjoy the narration as you read along I have great news for you. You can download this book for FREE just by signing up for a FREE 30-day audible trial.

FOR AUDIBLE UK:

FOR AUDIBLE US:

INTRODUCTION 8

SECTION 1: THE PLAN TO ORGANIZE YOUR LIFE 11

    Chapter 1: 14 Reasons Why It's Important to
Get Organized 12

    Chapter 2: The Top 5 Reasons for Disorganization 18

    Chapter 3: Goal-Setting 20

    Chapter 4: Developing Habits And Building A Routine .. 24

        Mastering the Force of Habit 25

        The Top 8 Routines of the Super-Organized 26

    Chapter 5: Be Consistent 28

        Why It's So Hard for You to Maintain Consistency? 29

        3 Steps to Help You Become Consistent 30

        The Importance of Planning Ahead 31

**SECTION 2: THE ORGANIZED MINDSET IN PRACTICE,
OR "CAN I BE TOO ORGANIZED?"** 33

    Chapter 1: Finding Balance 34

    Chapter 2: Prioritize 35

        What Is Prioritizing? 37

        Why is Prioritizing Important? 37

        How to Prioritize Tasks in 3 Steps 38

        3 Different Ways You Can Prioritize Tasks 39

Method 1: Prioritize Your List Again Based On When Things Need To Be Done. 39

Be Practical 41

Chapter 3: Hone Your Time Management Skills (As Well As Each 24-Hour Period) 41

A Call To Take Action: Prioritize Your Day! 43

Chapter 4: Time Management 43

What Is Time Management, and Why Is it Important? 44

How Can I Better Manage My Time? 46

Managing Distractions 49

Chapter 5: Monitor Your Progress 53

SECTION 3: ORGANIZE YOUR HOME 56

Chapter 1: Decluttering 57

How to Declutter in 3 Steps 57

Tips for Decluttering 59

Chapter 2: How to Organize Your Kitchen 64

Chapter 3: How to Organize Your Living Room 65

Chapter 4: How to Organize Your Bedroom 66

Chapter 5: How to Organize Your Closet 67

Chapter 6: How to Organize Your Bathroom 69

Chapter 7: Keeping Your Laundry Area Tidy 70

Chapter 8: How To Keep Your Home Organized for the Long Term — 71

A Call To Action: Start Organizing Your Home Today! — 71

SECTION 4: ORGANIZING OUTSIDE THE BOX — 72

Chapter 1: Organize Your Mind — 72

Chapter 2: Organize Your Money (And Become Wealthy) — 74

Chapter 3: Plan A Savings Strategy — 77

    Select Suitable Resources — 78

    Check Your Current Insurance Plan — 78

A Call To Action: Organizing Your Finances — 79

Chapter 4: Organize Your Relationships — 79

    5 Tips To Better Organize your Relationships — 80

A Call To Action: Decluttering Your Relationships — 81

    Five Steps You Can Take to Organize Your Social Life — 81

Chapter 5: Organize Your Health And Fitness — 84

A Call To Action: Be Honest About Your Health — 85

Chapter 6: Organize Your Work Life — 85

    Why It's So Important — 86

    The Positive Effects of Better Organization at Work — 86

    The 3 Essentials of Office Organization — 87

SECTION 5: PRACTICE ACCOUNTABILITY — 90

Chapter 1: 8 Ways to Stay Accountable and Organized in Your Life	91
Chapter 2: Mental Health, Accountability, Organization, and You	93

SECTION 6: ORGANIZING TOOLS **95**

Finances	96
Time	96
Planner	98
File Sharing and Storage	100
To-Do Lists	101
Reminders	102
Project Management	103
Organizing Software	104
Home	106
Kids Stuff	107

CONCLUSION **109**

INTRODUCTION

"Clutter is not just the stuff on your floor - it's anything that stands between you and the life you want to be living."

-PETER WALSH

Do you ever feel that there aren't enough resources at your disposal? Do you often run out of time, money, and gas? Do you constantly have a full trash can? Let me guess: you're in the typical position of being overworked and overstressed. You never seem to be able to sit back and take things easy. Good news: organization is the perfect remedy to help you regain control of your life.

Having a well-organized life is critical to achieving success in any area of your life. Being well-organized makes it easier to remain on top of work, and knowing where everything can be found reduces anxiety in the long run. The ability to maintain order in one's life may be developed with regular practice. If you follow the simple steps in this book, you'll soon be on your way to becoming a pro at organization.

True organizers aren't necessarily born that way; they work to establish productive routines that soon become second nature. So, if you consider yourself a person who is not very organized, you can still learn. If you are willing to study and practice what I share in this book, you will be well on your way to revolutionizing your life through organizing.

Instead of being discouraged and giving up too quickly, take things slowly and methodically as you learn to manage your life flawlessly.

Before we get started with the plan to organize your life, I want to make it clear that I am not arguing that a highly structured, military-like approach is always the best. There will always be those for whom it will never work, and that's okay. But if you desire a life that works on autopilot with minimal interruptions and unpredictable happenings, then organization is for you.
Being well-organized may help you:

- Get more done in less time
- Manage your energy and resources more effectively, and
- Feel less overwhelmed or burned out.

Being neat and tidy is a trait that will serve you well in the long term. You will be thankful to your future self if you take the time to be organized today!

It might seem like a constant juggling act trying to keep everything in order. Every time you react quickly enough to grab one ball (such as money, family obligations, or social opportunities), another one will come flying at you at full speed. Unfortunately, some balls will fall: there will be weeks in which sleep isn't a top priority; fast food is chosen over meal prepping, and shallow work is done instead of a thorough job.

An organizing framework will help you keep all areas of your life in order rather than randomly tossing chores and to-do lists into the air and hoping you catch them all.

In this book, we will discuss guidelines that will help you organize your life and maintain it that way. Then, we'll get into how you may use them in your everyday life, whether at work, at home, or even in your private life. We'll even take a look at the concept of organization in the terms of your health, fitness, money, and relationships.

The result of all this organization is increased productivity and less anxiety. Don't waste your life trying to juggle everything at once only to find yourself dropping more balls than you can catch.

SECTION 1: THE PLAN TO ORGANIZE YOUR LIFE

"Organization isn't about perfection it's about efficiency, reducing stress and clutter, saving time and money, and improving your overall quality of life".

- Christina Scalise

Rules are notorious for their rigidity and grimness. However, in practice, living by a set of rules may be liberating. Bear with me on this– having a plan of action helps us avoid the anguish of indecision and the analytical paralysis that comes with having too many options. But, that doesn't mean you can't enjoy the occasional spontaneous moments, so you may discover the pleasant surprises life has in store for you without losing your sanity. If you start following some basic principles and sticking to them, you may bring peace and order to your days and weeks, which can even free up time for more enjoyment.

This detailed, interactive book is full of tried-and-true suggestions for streamlining your life, adopting helpful routines, and growing as a person from the inside out. I'll show you the fundamentals of living a well-organized, purposeful life. Using these straightforward tools, you'll become an expert at anything from crossing items off your to-do lists to organizing your workspace.

The best method of organization is to plan and carry out short-term, intermediate-term, and long-term objectives. This book will assist you in achieving your creative objectives, whether they are professional or personal, by helping you develop more efficient routines and reasonable expectations for success. You'll receive helpful hints and recommendations for being organized in your daily life, tools for keeping track of time and completing tasks, and time-saving tips that will transform your life for the better.

If you want to make your own plan for success in life, this book will show you how to do it in a straightforward and uncomplicated way. To achieve your goals, you only need to keep moving forward in the proper direction. Thanks to this book, you now have a tremendous advantage in preparing for an organized life.

CHAPTER 1: 14 REASONS WHY IT'S IMPORTANT TO GET ORGANIZED

"Getting organized is a sign of self-respect."

-Gabrielle Bernstein

I have spent the greater part of the last several years cultivating routines and tools to help me become more efficient and productive in my time management and organizational endeavors. Setting daily objectives and organizing something as basic as your meals have had a huge influence on my life. I've also made a habit of constantly cleaning, organizing, and clearing out clutter so it doesn't have the chance to sneak up on me.

Consider these 14 benefits that accrue when you make an effort toward cleanliness and order:

Reason 1: Improved Quality of Life

Improve your quality of life by learning to better organize your schedule and assets. Fitting in all your accomplishments in addition to your exercise, career, family, and friends seems impossible. Fear not– keeping organized is the secret to success in achieving all your goals. You'll find that you can accomplish anything you want after you figure out how to properly organize your life.

Reason 2: Better Time Management

The one commodity most people now covet more than anything else is time. When you are more organized, it takes less time to maintain, tidy up, and arrange your space. That's great news because it means you'll have more time to devote to things that bring you the most satisfaction and results. Just think of all the time you've lost hunting for an item since you had no idea where you put it.

Keeping things in order has positive effects on your health that go beyond its aesthetic value. People who are well-organized know their responsibilities and how much time it will take to complete them. If you have an idea of what needs to be done but have no idea how long it will take, you should follow the lead of the well-organized and do what they do: keep track of the time they spend on each task. In doing this, you can see how your day typically goes and determine if there are any behaviors you want to alter.

Accordingly, the ability to arrange your daily activities will aid in time management. However, those who are consistently well-organized do more than just complete tasks on time. Because they are aware of where everything is as well as their priorities, they are able to focus on whichever endeavor they choose to engage in, making them most likely to be successful in life. So, clear the decks and put everything back where it belongs. Being disorganized might cause you to lose precious minutes, if not hours, each day as you search fruitlessly for essentials like your wallet.

Reason 3: Increased Efficiency

Being well-organized may help you get more done in less time. In this sense, your enhanced efficiency is a byproduct of your increased organization.

Think about it: if you're a well-organized person, you probably have the kind of time management skills that let you map out your days and weeks in advance. The core of productivity is pursuing better results while using the same effort or time. Those who know how to manage their time well are more likely to be more productive because of this.

Reason 4: Increased Energy

Having more energy is another upside to improving your life's organization. You'll feel refreshed and in charge once you learn how to manage your time, activities, and belongings well, making you more productive.

Having more energy naturally makes you happier. Moreover, when you're refreshed and confident in yourself, you'll be better equipped to handle challenging situations.

Reason 5: Better Diet

It may sound far-fetched, but scientific studies found a correlation between order and making better eating decisions. This impact has more to do with the mentality of a well-organized person and home than with the contents of the kitchen, but it is also applicable there. Placing healthy foods in an obvious location in the kitchen makes them more accessible. Also, being organized makes it possible to create more home-cooked meals, since meal planning/preparation is scheduled as opposed to regularly snacking or eating takeout.

Reason 6: Reduced Anxiety

It can be really frustrating if you often misplace your keys and constantly have trouble locating your footwear. Disorganization diverts attention from more pressing matters to the frustrating search for items that should never have been misplaced. A custom organizing system that takes into account how you live and the items you possess may make chaotic mornings a distant memory.

Reason 7: Improved Sleep Habits

Can being organized improve your ability to sleep? The more chaos you eliminate, the easier it will be to wind down and sleep well. The impact of seemingly small everyday actions, such as placing clean clothing in their proper drawers and keeping a laundry basket or hamper for soiled items can be significant. Imagine if your precious sleep time wouldn't be disrupted as you stay up in a bid to catch up with unfinished but pressing chores!

Reason 8: Reduced Stress and Depression

There are undoubtedly mental health consequences to living in a house that is perpetually chaotic and disorganized. Anxiety and depression are common when daily stresses are added to those dealing with life's difficulties and interpersonal conflicts. That goes double for individuals who are predisposed to mental health concerns. Being organized has been shown to reduce stress, increase mental clarity, and lessen the likelihood of feeling overwhelmed.

Taking charge of your environment is an excellent way to protect yourself from experiencing depressive and anxious episodes. There are lots of things we have no say over in this world, but you can take charge of your workspace and personal space by keeping it perfectly organized.

Reason 9: More Time

Being well-organized has many advantages, but one of my favorite benefits is the time it frees up to spend on your own interests. In order to pursue our passions, we all need more leisure time. Time is squandered on chaos and disorganization, but we don't see it that way until we embrace order and organization. Just making this one mental adjustment can have profound effects on your life. Consider the time you squander every day trying to keep up with your own disarray, rather than spending time doing what you actually enjoy.

Reason 10: Increased Creativity

When you're consistently organized, you feel revitalized on all levels, from the physical to the mental, paving the way for your imagination to go wild. Being well-organized means being available for those "aha!" moments when inspiration hits. It involves organizing your environment in such a way that inspiration can flow freely whenever you need it. That way, when you get into your creative flow state, your actual surroundings are ready to accommodate you, and you can get to work right away.

Reason 11: More Flexibility

When things are relatively calm, you are in a better position to deal with any unexpected developments that may arise. If you have a well-established routine at home and a reliable set of procedures in place, you'll be better equipped to adapt swiftly to the inevitable changes that occur when you least expect them. If you have some fundamental structures in place, you can delegate responsibility for your house or workplace to someone else if necessary.

Reason 12: Improved Health

The question running through your mind now is likely - 'How does this work?' In order to take better care of yourself and your well-being, you need to increase your productivity and stop spending time wallowing in organizational turmoil. If you don't waste an hour every day looking for your keys, you'll have more time to devote to healthy habits like eating and exercising.

Reason 13: Increased Self-Esteem

The key to finding anything quickly and efficiently is organization. It's much easier for you to complete things on time, stick to schedules, and arrive punctually. Consequently, your efficiency and output will improve. And gradually, that internal monologue starts to change its melody. Those doubts and questions about your ability to get things done will be replaced by confidence and the knowledge that you've got it! You will feel confident in your abilities and excited about the future. Your self-esteem will skyrocket.

Reason 14: Enhanced Relationships

Relationships with family, friends, and colleagues can also be negatively impacted by one person's poor time management and unwillingness to declutter their living space. Tension and frustration can grow from habitually arriving late and failing to keep commitments. If you keep your schedule in order, you won't miss any appointments and will always meet your deadlines.

After reviewing some of the important benefits of being well-organized, you're probably curious to learn more about the specifics of becoming organized.

CHAPTER 2: THE TOP 5 REASONS FOR DISORGANIZATION

"The hallmark of a disorganized individual is that they never finish what they start."

-Matthew Snider

There is no quick fix for getting organized and increasing productivity. You can't expect to get better at organizing without first identifying the root of the problem. If you ask ten different people what they believe is the cause of their disorganization, you will most likely hear ten different explanations. Identifying the root of your disorganization is essential to making progress and it improves your chances of becoming and staying organized. So keep that in mind as you work to make changes.

Reason 1: Distraction

One thing many of us wish for is the ability to concentrate on a single activity from inception to completion. There are physiological causes of distraction, and there are also environmental causes. If your cubicle entrance is causing you to spend more time watching people than working, move your desk so that you are not facing it. You'll be able to concentrate better and be less distracted if you turn one of your shoulders toward the door. List out things you constantly get distracted by and make a plan to eliminate the distraction.

Reason 2: Procrastination

Procrastination is something that you are already aware of if you are someone who tends to put things off until later. If it seems you're always putting off tasks until the last minute, your reason for disorganization might just be procrastination. The only issue is that there is just too much to accomplish the next day, so either nothing gets done or something important falls through the gap. If you tend to put things off, try rewarding yourself with your favorite treat or activity if you're able to get the task completed right away.

Reason 3: Multitasking

Well-organized people often believe in their abilities as expert multitaskers. However, scientific evidence from multiple studies over the past ten years strongly contradicts this. Some studies have found that multitasking reduces productivity by 20-40% for the average individual. As a result, multitaskers clean up messes while attempting to be productive, which can add more confusion and chaos to their lives.

Reason 4: Unexpected Changes

Change is a constant in our lives, but we don't always pause to consider how it can affect our capacity to maintain order and stay on schedule. You might be going through a difficult time in your life, including a breakup, the loss of a loved one, a wedding, the arrival of a new baby, etc. The sum of these factors will have a significant impact on your life if you are not a naturally organized person.

Reason 5: Indecision

The inability to make choices is a major contributor to clutter at home and in the workplace. One of the most common causes of chaos in the workplace or private life is the inability to make decisions. Consider the items currently occupying your dining room table, as well as the piles of paper and books that sit beneath your desk and on top of your cabinets. The majority of distractions signify a decision that hasn't been made.

CHAPTER 3: GOAL-SETTING

"I have a motto on my bedroom wall: 'Obstacles are what you see when you take your eye off the goal.' Giving up is not my style. I just want to do something that's worthwhile."

– Chris Burke

Do you tend to make the same New Year's resolutions year after year? Do you keep telling yourself that you'll get that thing done, only to abandon it again later? People often set goals, then give up on them or fail to reach them. They then set the same goals again, this time with a newfound but short-lived determination to succeed.

However, you have the power to end this negative spiral with the three most commonly asked questions about setting goals.

Question 1: What is goal setting?

A common reason why people fail to achieve their objectives is that they fail to differentiate between their goals and their more casual, everyday efforts to develop themselves. The mere act of committing to a daily running routine does not constitute a well-considered objective. Let's review the meaning of creating goals to become more organized.

The first step in making goals is to be specific about what you want to do, whether learning a new skill or finishing a project. The next step is to design a strategy to realize that goal and put forth effort until it is accomplished.

For example, if you're tired of jogging aimlessly, a more meaningful objective might be to sign up for a training program in preparation for a specific race, such as the half marathon held on Thanksgiving Day.

Question 2: So why is it crucial to set goals?

You may steer the course of your life and career by setting and working toward certain objectives. Setting these goals helps clearly direct your efforts in a clear path. All of your choices and moves should help you get closer to your objectives. Having a plan to achieve your goals keeps you on track, boosts your happiness, and provides huge benefits for your career. Goal-setting is the process of imagining a better future for oneself or one's organization. The next step is to put in the effort necessary to achieve your goals.

Question 3: How do I get started setting goals?

Why do we set goals if they are supposed to be essential but we never seem to be able to achieve them? It's mostly due to the fact that we do not plan the actions necessary to achieve the goal.

When you set goals for yourself, you have to consider not only the final destination but also the steps you'll take to get there. Check out these guidelines to get started.

1. **Visualize the outcome you seek.**

    Before you commit to a goal, think about the answers to the following questions about what you want to achieve:

    - Is it something you really want to accomplish?
    - Is it worth spending time on? It might not be worthwhile to try if you can't commit to giving it a solid chunk of your time.

You may find it challenging to accomplish your objectives if you make a lengthy list of them and try to work on them simultaneously. Use the preceding questions to zero in on the few objectives that truly matter at the moment.

2. Make sure your objectives are SMART.

When you have a clear idea of what it is that you want, the next step is to evaluate whether or not your objectives are SMART:

- Specific
- Measurable
- Attainable
- Realistic
- Time-bound

The first step in achieving a SMART goal is to formulate a clear, well-defined objective that can be measured against a standard. You'll have a better chance of succeeding if your objective is clear and well-defined. Don't worry- we'll talk about SMART things a few more times as we work towards greater organization!

3. Put your goals on paper

Putting your aspirations on paper transforms them from a huge concept in your head into something concrete and attainable. After you've written down your objectives, keep them in a place where you'll see them often. This may be your bathroom mirror or the wall next to your desk at work.

This strategy will serve as a daily reminder to keep pushing toward your objectives. When you are listing your objectives, make sure to do so with full optimism that you can complete these tasks, so that you remain motivated to achieve them.

4. Formulate a strategy

Unfortunately, many people set an objective without ever devising a strategy for how they'll actually achieve it. You should describe both your long-term goal and the specific steps you will take to achieve it. Making an action plan in this way involves engaging a new area of the brain, making it more likely that the goals will stick in your memory.

5. Develop a schedule

It is important to be as consistent as possible with the dates you have chosen. Having a deadline in mind can help keep you on track to achieve your objective on time.

Utilizing a time management app as a component of your action plan might assist you in better visualizing the roles, actions, and milestones necessary to reach your objective. I've included a few helpful options towards the end of this book to get you started.

6. Take Action

After careful preparation and planning, the next step is to put your strategy into motion. You didn't come this far without keeping the end in mind, did you? Your actions should build upon one another, leading you closer and closer to success.

7. Take stock of where you are and how far you've come

Staying motivated is essential if you want to reach your target. You might want to organize a weekly review for yourself, in which you track your progress and verify that you are on track with your plans. If you can get a glimpse of the final goal, you'll be more driven to keep going. Don't let falling behind schedule derail you; instead, make the required modifications and keep going.

8. Get started with your goal-setting now!

Setting goals and working toward them is an effective way to achieve your objectives. It has the potential to fire up your drive and get you where you want to go. A goal-setting method helps define detailed, timely, and achievable goals.

Plan out your steps to improve your performance and follow them to ensure success. Following these steps will help you not only set goals for getting organized but help you arrange the goal-setting process into something you can accomplish. As you become a more organized person, you'll discover the many ways in which being organized impacts your life. Don't believe me? Keep reading!

CHAPTER 4: DEVELOPING HABITS AND BUILDING A ROUTINE

The trick to success is to choose the right habit and bring just enough discipline to establish it.

-Gary Keller and Jay Papasan

Here's the thing about organization that few people discuss or recognize: it's a habit.

This might be discouraging, since forming new habits and breaking old ones can be challenging. In my opinion, it's great, because you can aim for success and model your own behavior after that of highly organized people.

When you're at a loss for how to gain a sense of mastery over your day, a daily routine might be a lifesaver. Those who have trouble keeping to schedules but would benefit from having a more organized day might also benefit from establishing less strict routines.

We could all benefit from being more organized, but did you know that it's your habits, not your to-do list, that will make the biggest difference in decluttering your life? Practicing these routines can help you become more organized in your daily life.

Mastering the Force of Habit

The goal is to make the most efficient use of your limited daily energy reserves. However, it's likely that your time and energy are being diverted away from the more significant undertakings that need constant focus and effort to complete. You may save time and effort by harnessing the power of habit and applying it where it will have the most impact on your productivity. Those who take pride in their ability to think outside the box may find it comforting to know that incorporating some routines and habits into their day frees them up to focus on creative tasks when they arise.

Think about the first things you do when you wake up in the morning. Maybe you brush your teeth, wash your face, take a shower, etc. These are now ingrained habits that you perform automatically every morning. While you are doing them, your mind is preoccupied with something else, like listening to the radio or planning out your day, so you don't think about them at all. They need essentially zero cognitive effort on your part. Some parts of your workday can be boiled down to something as easy as brushing your teeth. Over time, these activities have become habits– things we do automatically without thinking.

Currently, activities like organizing your home and keeping track of your belongings drain too much of your time and effort without providing nearly the same benefits. They compete with other obligations for your time, forcing you to make tough choices about when to get things done and causing unnecessary stress when they go undone. Incorporating new routines into your day may take time, but once they become a habit like brushing your teeth, you'll stay organized without having to think too much about what you're doing.

The Top 8 Routines of the Super-Organized

Being well-organized isn't only a skill you develop. To be honest, it might seem like a difficult process at first. However, if you continue to live an orderly life, you may come to view it less as a duty and more as a mentality. For instance, you may decide to start planning every aspect of your daily life in advance. A moment will come, though, when your systems and rituals become ingrained in your routine and your mind will have adapted to them to the point where they are habits. If you've reached this point, you may consider yourself an organized person.

So, without further ado, let's dive into the 8 routines that highly organized individuals always follow. Have no fear: you've got this!

1. They always think ahead to the next day.

The end of the day is a great opportunity to think ahead to the next day. Make a new list of things to accomplish every day!

2. They work off of a carefully crafted list of tasks.

Sticking to a to-do list is like relying on a lifeline while you're drowning in chaos. Know your tasks and stick to your goals!

3. They prioritize.

Which task has the closest deadline and is critical to success? Do it first! Always keep your priorities in mind. Whatever can be put off until later should be, and the unpleasant- yet often important- tasks should be tackled first.

4. They implement timers and reminders.

Most of us just cannot afford to make mistakes in time and money management. Your odds of successfully dodging a big problem will greatly improve if you equip yourself with as many organizational tools as possible. Make sure you take care of your responsibilities on time by setting alarms, reminders, and any other tools you may find useful.

5. They integrate wiggle room in the case of last-minute list revisions.

You're in the middle of your normal day when your mom suddenly contacts you with an urgent situation. Is your schedule flexible enough to accommodate this last-minute change? It's imperative that you create a series of deadlines that accommodate changes and emergencies.

6. They consistently take time out for themselves.

It's not about being a slave to your schedule. Once you have begun decluttering your home and organizing your life, you'll find there's always room to make some time for yourself. Do something relaxing like reading a book, watching a movie, or working out at the gym to help you recenter and feel refreshed.

7. In every case, they make sure that everything is completed.

This is the holy grail of staying organized. Finish whatever you start. A person who is disorganized always seems to have things left undone.

8. They leave no place for clutter.

Clutter, as was discussed before, is detrimental to your success. Give it no breathing room on your turf! We'll address clutter directly in the next section to help you better adapt to a life with no unnecessary messes.

Mastering each of these techniques will take some time, which is where goal-setting can help you. Be patient with yourself, and don't get too upset if you find yourself unable to magically make everything change all at once. Set goals, and allow yourself to work towards them. Eventually, you'll turn those goals into long-lasting behaviors.

CHAPTER 5: BE CONSISTENT

Does this sound familiar? You set your sights on a certain goal, such as a more fit body, a clutter-free home, more fulfilling relationships, or a more robust skill set. You decide to enroll in a personal development course, start playing the piano, clear out a part of your house, read a book, or go to the gym.

For the first week or so, you devote every waking moment to your newfound passion because you're so driven to achieve your goal. However, you eventually begin to neglect your practice. You miss today. You miss five days. Before you know it, you've stopped going to the gym, returned to old habits, left your home in shambles, and forgotten about your piano. And thus the process repeats itself.

That's pretty much how many of us spend our days. Our inconsistency is a major source of distress for everyone involved. Even though we've learned the hard way that consistency is the key to growth in any aspect of life, we keep on stumbling. One thing you never fail to do is begin an endeavor and abandon it before its completion. Despite your self-flagellation, there is still a chance. The only way to get out of these ruts is to figure out what causes us to repeat the same mistakes over and over again, and only then can we hope to succeed in breaking the cycle.

Why It's So Hard for You to Maintain Consistency?

First off, you have been inconsistent because you are concerned primarily with the final product rather than the steps involved in reaching that result. That doesn't mean the end isn't important, but it's counterproductive to put too much emphasis on it. Why? Simply put, if you're hoping for a really exciting ending, it's probably not going to come about without a lot of effort and dedication. Most of us lack the stamina to put in the work required to achieve our goals if we don't have any processes in place to aid us.

Incorporating regularity into your strategy is essential if you want to see positive results. But first, we must establish the scope of the project with the goal-setting process we just examined. This strategy has four components:

- Specifying the result (e.g., "I want to get my office in order").
- Finding the overarching "why" behind your goal (e.g. "By improving my mental and physical health, I will be better able to care for my family's material, spiritual, and emotional needs").
- Goal setting is the process of establishing milestones that, when reached, will lead you to the intended result (e.g. organizing one room in 10 days).
- Creating methods to reach these objectives.

Because it is fundamental to the development of consistency, I will concentrate on the fourth step of the plan- goal setting. You see, most well-intended plans fail at this fourth stage.

3 Steps to Help You Become Consistent

Consider these steps to help guide you through the goal-setting process, which can help you establish a consistent pattern on your path to organization.

Step 1: Focus on the Now

The term "being present" refers to a state of mental concentration in which one gives one's undivided attention to the activity one is now performing. This involves restraining our natural inclination to squander time, effort, and resources fretting over things of the past or future that we can do nothing to alter. For instance, as a writer, you can't focus on your work unless you eliminate distractions. For you, that may involve getting up before the rest of the family and keeping your phone away. Even if you have some negative thoughts flooding your mind as you go through the day, focus on doing the work still.

Step 2: Prepare for "*The Dip*"

Most of us start on new ventures assuming that getting where we want to go will be simple and uncomplicated. Incredibly, we believe this even when we know otherwise from experience.

Seth Godin writes in his book The Dip that the middle portion of any worthwhile endeavor is inevitably chaotic. He terms this less-than-enjoyable part of the process "the Dip." The fact that the Dip often occurs after an early period of success just adds to the difficulty it presents. This acts as a filter, separating the quitters from those who go on to achieve great success. The act of quitting is not necessarily negative. The book's main objective is to teach the reader how to recognize and discard non-essential pursuits. Knowing the Dip is coming will help you realize that you need an action plan to deal with it.

Step 3: Remember the Fundamentals

Most of us would rather skip the boring, foundational stages of any endeavor and jump straight to the fun, advanced parts. It's easy to get disheartened by more advanced tactics and plans if we haven't spent enough time mastering the basics. You simply can't get your life in order if you don't cover the basics of time management and prioritization. Despite their significance, our chaotic lives can cause us to lose sight of the fundamentals we need to succeed.

The Importance of Planning Ahead

"An hour of planning can save you 10 hours of doing."

– Dale Carnegie

The Collins English Dictionary defines planning as "the process of choosing in detail how to achieve something before you really start to do it." On the other hand, "organizing" is defined as "the action or ability of coordinating people and events."

The logical first step in organizing and implementing anything is to come up with a strategy for doing so. After all, it's difficult to coordinate the many stages of an endeavor or carry it out in practice if you haven't figured out how to accomplish it in the first place.

By setting goals and creating an overall strategy for success, you'll have a greater ability to hold yourself accountable for each step of your progress. Goal setting allows us to carefully consider the steps we'll need to take to succeed, from getting the clutter off the dining table to understanding how to better prioritize our personal lives.

SECTION 2: THE ORGANIZED MINDSET IN PRACTICE, OR "CAN I BE TOO ORGANIZED?"

"Nobody ever said, 'I regret organizing my house.'"

— **Alejandra Costello**

Maintaining a tidy and uncluttered space is a habit worth cultivating. Some people see it as the key to solving all of their issues. On the other hand, obsessive neatness can be harmful if it becomes a habit. Avoid trying to exert too much control and letting your perfectionism get the best of you.

If you realize you're adding to your stress, bothering those around you, or spending more time planning than working: Stop. Relax and reevaluate the situation. Try to find a happy medium where your ways of organizing help you and the people around you and are easy to use.

Also, have a flexible mindset. Plans might fail even if they're well thought out, so it's a good idea to be able to adapt to whatever the day throws at you. Make sure there is enough wiggle room in your calendar in case you have an emergency.

CHAPTER 1: FINDING BALANCE

"In all aspects of our lives, balance is key. Doing one thing too much can cause upset, like the old saying goes, everything in moderation is the secret!"

– Catherine Pulsifer

Balance is often sacrificed in our pursuit of efficiency and perfection. You're not getting any sleep because you're too busy working. Instead of spending the weekend with your pals, you decide to cram for your approaching midterm.

While this approach may produce immediate results, its long-term effects of stress, fatigue, and apathy are not pretty.

You've reached the point of burnout if your goal has taken over your life. Even if you're dedicated to your work and passionate about becoming the best at what you do, it's important to schedule downtime to recharge. Work out as hard as an athlete, but don't forget how important rest, recovery, and self-care are for long-term success.

To help you get started on a balanced path, here are a few tips:
- Don't put undue stress on yourself by working excessive hours.
- Consider the positive impact of exercise on your mood and schedule it regularly.
- Think about starting a gratitude journal, meditation, or a combination of these things.
- Get together with loved ones to keep you centered.
- Isolate yourself and unwind with a movie or book when you start feeling stressed.
- Try not to pull all-nighters unless absolutely necessary.

- Take regular breaks to catch your breath, but also schedule in some lengthier sabbaticals. It's recommended that you take a week off from work at least twice a year. Schedule annual vacations to give yourself time to rest and regroup.
- You should put forth your best effort during the day, but you should also make sure to leave work on time.
- Turn off your devices over the weekend and reconnect with loved ones.
- Do not send or respond to emails beyond normal business hours.

Staying energized is essential so that you can be there for the people who depend on you in your professional and personal life. Maintaining balance in all areas of your life can help you devote your time and energy to pursuits that will benefit you.

CHAPTER 2: PRIORITIZE

"Time management is an oxymoron. Time is beyond our control, and the clock keeps ticking regardless of how we lead our lives. Priority management is the answer to maximizing the time we have."

– John C. Maxwell

We touched on prioritization earlier, but it bears a deeper dive. The ability to prioritize is extremely valuable but is rarely explicitly taught. Prioritization is, in every regard, a life skill. Just as we are to teach good table manners to children, we should teach prioritization too. Then many of us could avoid the struggle with the chaos that comes with adulting and building careers for the first time.

Prioritizing will allow you to make the most of everything, especially your workday. Contrary to what many have come to believe, "busy" does not always mean productive. Alas, what truly matters is the effectiveness of our work and how efficiently we use our time. The appearance of busyness does not necessarily mean you're using your time well. But this is the 21st century, and with so much going on in our personal lives, work lives, and the world, it can be difficult to set priorities.

At the beginning of each new year, you probably set some goals for yourself, such as devoting more time to loved ones, discovering your true calling in life, or launching a new business. But somehow, gradually, you began to ignore or totally forget those goals. Those who remember them are often plagued with the challenge of creating time and maximizing resources.

But no matter what our goals are or how busy we are, we can not neglect essentials like taking care of our children or showing up for work. The problem, then, is that there are obstacles all around us, preventing us from achieving our goals. For instance, it's hard to say no to a high-paying work opportunity, even if it means sacrificing time with family. The time you spend on mundane tasks like checking emails, doing errands, and browsing social media sites adds up faster than you might like to admit. That's why it's so important to figure out what matters most to you and then develop the skills to make that a top priority.

So, what is the bottom line here? Putting your beliefs into practice begins with mastering time management. You have to decide to take the long view and work toward your ideal future. In addition, you have to be able to prioritize effectively and realize your loftiest ambitions versus your most realistic goals.

What Is Prioritizing?

The process of prioritizing involves evaluating the significance and timeliness of various activities, events, and objects. Priority tasks are accomplished before less critical ones, so you may want to look at each task in light of everything you need to accomplish. Learning to prioritize your work or the tasks at hand will help you get more done in less time.

With proper prioritization, you may find that certain seemingly essential chores don't need to be dealt with right away. Again, if you want to get more out of each workday, you need to learn how to prioritize things instead of treating everything as equally important. A constant state of activity does not guarantee achievement. By organizing the functions from most critical to least important, prioritization systems guarantee that all work done is productive.

Why is Prioritizing Important?

Developing expert prioritization skills can completely transform your life, especially in terms of relieving the anxiety that comes from worrying about not finishing a job by the deadline. You may strike a better balance between your professional and personal life if you learn to control your time more effectively. And it is a fact that the more effectively you use your time, the more progress you'll make on all of your tasks and chores.

A person's motivation and ability to set priorities are the two most important factors in their level of productivity. When you don't properly prioritize your work, you end up expending a lot of time and effort on projects that don't really matter. If you don't know how to set priorities, you'll always have difficulty finishing everything on time, which will just add to your stress levels. Prioritizing is essential to maximize productivity.

How to Prioritize Tasks in 3 Steps

Now that you know the importance of prioritizing, especially in terms of productivity, it is time to put your plans in motion. Here are some fundamental tips for figuring out which of your tasks is more important than the rest:

Step 1: Make A Checklist Of Everything You Need To Do

Step one is to make a comprehensive list of everything you need to accomplish in a single day. You don't need to worry about the sequence of your assignments right now; you just need to get everything written down. Yes, work requests can come in from several places via various methods, and it may not be easy to deal with them when they do. But creating room to cater to unforeseen requests will definitely help.

Step 2: Sort the Items on Your List in the Order of Importance

As a further step, verify each task's level of significance or urgency. Not completing a pivotal step in your process by the due date will have far-reaching effects on your project. The best strategy to prioritize your work is to compare and contrast individual jobs. Prioritize the jobs on the list from step one by assigning a number value between zero and ten, based on the things that need to be completed immediately. The task with the highest number is given the highest priority, followed by the task with the next highest.

Step 3: Consider How Much Time You Spend on Each Activity

It is possible to still have a lengthy list of things to do after prioritizing them. Implement the famous Ivy Lee Method to determine how much time you spend on each activity.

- Make a list of productive things to do the next day. Make sure you don't have more than six tasks to complete.
- Rank the activities in order of importance.

- By the start of the next day, give your full attention to the most important task until it's completed. Don't skip this step; finish it up before moving on.
- Continue working in this fashion on the remaining tasks. If you have work left over at the end of the day, add it to tomorrow's list of things to do.

This process has been helping top performers organize their tasks for over a hundred years, and it might just help you, too!

3 Different Ways You Can Prioritize Tasks

Method 1: Prioritize Your List Again Based On When Things Need To Be Done.

The tasks themselves are not the primary focus of the prioritization process. Time management is also a key part of this process. After prioritizing the list, work on the items with the closest due dates first. When you get the most important and urgent task out of the way, you gain the motivation and momentum to keep going to finish the rest.

If the request doesn't include a due date, you'll need to establish one. Time multipliers are the most effective tool for creating realistic deadlines. An approach or tool that frees up more of your time, in the long run, is called a "time multiplier." Methods like these can help you save up more time for when you really need it. Time management considerations made today can yield benefits tomorrow.

Method 2: Prioritize Your Work Based on How Hard It Is.

After prioritizing tasks by the due date, you can reorder the list based on how much time and effort each item will take to complete. The more time-consuming jobs should be prioritized above the less time-consuming ones.

Are you familiar with the phrase, "Eat the frog?" Well, "eating the frog" is a way to manage your time by doing the hardest but most important task first thing in the morning. According to a quote by Mark Twain, if you eat a live frog as soon as you wake up each morning, it will probably be the worst thing that happens to you all day. This will allow you to face the rest of the day with confidence. The "frog" represents the most difficult or crucial assignment you face. Your procrastination risk is highest with this one if you don't take action. Therefore, "eat that frog" is another way of saying, "If you have two chickens to fry, fry the biggest one first." Discipline yourself to get started right away and keep going until the job is done.

This provides the impetus and motivation to carry out the remaining tasks. If you think you'll be more productive if you do a task early, you'd better delay it. Start with the toughest activities and work your way down to the less taxing ones. Getting something done first thing in the morning can do wonders for your mood throughout the day.

Method 3: Let Go Of Unnecessary Commitments.

You should be adaptable during the prioritization process. There is no way of knowing what will happen in the future, and that is a hard fact. You should avoid the sunk cost fallacy because no matter what you spend your time on, you can never get it back. The "sunk cost fallacy" is a psychological effect in which someone puts time and effort into a task and then feels compelled to finish it. Allow yourself to leave some tasks unfinished, especially if there is no reason to devote energy to them. If you have a bunch of "useless" tasks on your to-do list, consider the consequences of not doing them. You may find you've started something you don't need to finish.

Be Practical

The goal of prioritization is to increase productivity, but if you ask too much of yourself, it will backfire! Interruptions such as meetings and phone calls might cause tasks to run longer than expected.

Once you learn to prioritize, you'll be able to stop worrying about how much you should get done and start concentrating on how much you can actually get done in a given day. Understanding how much you can get done in a day is an important part of setting priorities. Be realistic and honest with yourself about the tasks you can complete in a day. Remember, never ask too much of yourself. Know your limits and you'll do just fine!

CHAPTER 3: HONE YOUR TIME MANAGEMENT SKILLS (AS WELL AS EACH 24-HOUR PERIOD)

During what percentage of the day do you feel totally in charge? Are you wasting precious hours on pursuits that you don't care about? Do you usually work toward your own goals or those of others? How can you cut out unnecessary things? Approximately how much time do you waste daily? Describe your perfect day. How much of your time is spent on tasks that could be delegated or automated?

What you do with your time has a direct impact on whether or not you reach your goals. Time disappears and moves swiftly until you give it direction. All of a sudden, you're out of time and wondering where those hours and minutes went. Time will seem to slow down after you get organized. Once you understand how your time is spent, you can focus more on the here and now. Time will be your own to manipulate any way you like. Instead of time controlling you, you'll be in command. You'll be astounded at how much time you have. That's right; our time here on Earth is limited. However, we have the means to slow it down and feel it.

Now, how did your day go today? Seriously. Take a moment to think back on what you accomplished today. Did you display the qualities you hope to acquire? Where would you be– realistically– if you had to relive today's schedule every day for the next year? How different would your typical day need to be from today if you were to achieve your goals and dreams? What could a typical day look like for you while you work toward your goals? Take a step toward creating your ideal life by visualizing your perfect day. Take the time to really consider how your daily patterns impact your time spent working towards your goals.

Which habits must you maintain daily to realize your ideal lifestyle? There may be a few obstacles preventing you from having what you might consider a perfect day right now, but are you making progress toward that goal? Determine what constitutes a perfect day for yourself based on your personal standards of happiness. Only you can decide what constitutes a successful life for yourself.

Here is a breakdown of what I consider an efficient day:

- Sleep for the recommended 8 hours.
- Eat a mindful diet consisting of eating only the healthiest foods, including more fruits and veggies to your diet and trying to cut down on carbs.
- Exercise for 30-60 minutes.
- Prayer and meditation for 15-30 minutes (no smartphone).
- Reading time to grow your mind 1-3 hours (no smartphone).
- Five to eight hours of work.
- Two to three hours with the family.

What sequence these things take place in is irrelevant. For most of us, one day is never like the next. But after completing all of these tasks, I still have nearly four hours left over to do things like check my email, eat, drive, perform acts of service, get sidetracked, chat on the phone with friends, and whatever else might come up.

From both good and bad experiences, I have learned that the mood I'm in when I first open my eyes in the morning has a profound impact on the rest of my day. The remainder of my day goes tremendously better if I get up on time and with a plan, which is usually before 6 o'clock.

Now, describe the perfect day for you. Is your perfect day something you experience frequently? Where would you be a year from now if you lived your perfect day every day? In five years, where do you see yourself?

A Call To Take Action: Prioritize Your Day!

- Imagine for a moment what your perfect day would entail.
- Create a schedule of your ideal day's events.
- Continue to keep a record of your day-to-day activities. Time tracking and self-awareness will open your eyes to where you need to reduce time and where you need to schedule more time.

CHAPTER 4: TIME MANAGEMENT

"For every minute spent organizing, an hour is earned."

– Benjamin Franklin

There are 24 hours in a day, no matter who you are. Although, you've probably noticed that some people do appear to be more productive than others. What is their little secret?

Time management is how you consistently schedule, prioritize, and complete tasks. While you can't add more hours to your day, if you learn to manage your time well, you'll find that you'll be far more content, healthier, and productive. While the specifics of your life will have the greatest impact on your ability to manage time, there are some universal principles that can be applied to anyone's professional and personal life to help them become more productive and efficient time managers.

You need to know what successful time management is and how to manage time if you want to make the most of your day.

What Is Time Management, and Why Is it Important?

To put it simply, time management is the art of scheduling one's actions to get the most out of one's day. One of the main benefits of time management is that it allows workers to accomplish more in less time.

Most of us are terrible at giving each work assignment the time and attention they need, so mastering the art of time management might have a significant influence on your career. So, let's quickly examine the advantages being aware of how you use your time can provide:

- Improved Organizational Skills
- Increased efficiency
- Reduced stress levels
- Healthier work-life balance

On the other hand, if you don't manage your time well, bad things could happen. Are you familiar with any of these tragedies?

- Missed deadlines
- Low quality of job performance
- Elevated levels of stress
- Forced inequity in the workplace
- Exhaustion and burnout

Workers who have mastered the art of time management are in a position to make the most of their working hours. People are more productive, enthusiastic, and resistant to burnout when things are going as planned. So, it makes sense to spend some time learning how to manage your time if you want to move up in your chosen field.

Some people always appear to have enough time to do what they set out to achieve, while others are always juggling a number of different responsibilities. To accomplish all that is desired, one must learn to manage their time wisely. Effective time management requires a wide range of abilities such as:

- Maintaining a sense of order
- How to set priorities for getting things done
- Clarifying your objectives
- Effective verbal and non-verbal communication skills
- A well-organized daily schedule
- Learning to delegate responsibilities
- Efficiently dealing with stressful situations

How Can I Better Manage My Time?

You should use these potent time management ideas now that you understand their significance. Let's examine some time-management strategies and apps that might help you achieve your goals quickly and efficiently.

Sticking to a Daily Schedule

Make use of a digital planner. Technology has made it much easier to keep track of important dates and events. Use your phone's or computer's calendar feature. Take the time to jot down your daily activities, such as work and school hours, appointments, and other commitments. Prepare yourself by establishing a system of reminders. Set phone or email alerts to remind you of upcoming commitments.

If you like the satisfaction of crossing things off your to-do list or if you find it easier to see your list, a paper calendar is a great alternative.

Find the times of day when you are able to get the most done.

People have varying degrees of efficiency throughout the day. To maximize productivity, it might be helpful to identify the times of day when you are at your best: alert and motivated. Take advantage of your peak productivity times; for instance, if you're at your best first thing in the morning, schedule most of your work for then. The evening is a great time to unwind and focus on self-care.

Finding your energy peaks might be a process that takes time. Take a week or two and record how much energy and concentration you have at certain times during the day. You may use this information to determine when you are most likely to get work done.

Making a plan for the day early in the morning or the previous day might be helpful. If you want to get things done, you should start doing so as soon as possible after waking up. Don't forget about your responsibilities at work, as well as your social commitments and errands.

Plan both substantial and small diversions from your daily routine and stick to them.

Plan for pauses and disruptions. Even the most dedicated worker needs occasional rest breaks in order to maintain productivity. There are times when diversions and interruptions should be welcomed. Scheduling such breaks from routine work might be helpful. Consequently, your day will be less likely to get completely consumed by interruptions.

Think about making regular habits, like taking a one-hour lunch break every day at 1 p.m if possible and watching a half-hour of TV every night to unwind from the day.

Small distractions might be strategically placed in the course of regular activities. Take, for instance, a scenario in which you are writing a research article, you can give yourself ten minutes to visit Instagram for every 500 words you write. This would motivate you to accomplish tasks faster.

Utilize your day off productively and get things done.

It's the weekend, a time for pleasure and relaxation, so don't overdo it. Consider the kinds of minor errands that build up over days off and make Mondays a challenge.

For instance, to have fewer unread messages waiting for you when you return to work on Monday, you may, for instance, briefly check and review your emails over the weekend and send a couple only if your workplace permits it. You could also just mark the ones that need quick attention on Monday and move them to the top of the list.

Maintain a regular bedtime schedule.

A reliable sleep routine is essential for effective time management. In order to stay alert and productive upon waking, it's important to get plenty of rest on a regular basis. Whether on weekdays or weekends, try to keep your bedtime and waking time somewhat constant. In time, your body will adjust to your new schedule and you'll feel sleepy when it's bedtime and refreshed when it's wake-up time.

Take care of the most pressing matters first.

If you can, get the most important things done first. With that out of the way, you can relax and enjoy the rest of your day knowing it has already been a success.

Make sure you're working in an appropriate setting

The conditions in which you perform your work might have a significant impact on your efficiency. There are no hard and fast regulations about the ideal workplace, so feel free to create an atmosphere that best suits you. Put yourself in an upbeat and enthusiastic frame of mind by surrounding yourself with motivating artwork and other décor. These emotions will serve to keep you focused and efficient in your work.

It's possible, for instance, that a specific painter serves as a source of motivation for you. Purchase some prints of their work and proudly display them on your walls. If you have the option of where you do your job, it's best to pick somewhere quiet and peaceful.

Managing Distractions

Put the phone on silent mode when you are not actively using it. Using a phone may be a major time sink that prevents you from getting anything done. While checking Twitter and Facebook may seem like it takes very little time, people log in to them more frequently. When procrastination strikes and you go for your phone, you'll be confronted with nothing but a blank screen.

If your job requires you to keep your phone on at all times, move it to the other side of the room. You won't be as inclined to check your phone if you have to work a little more to get to it. Disabling non-work-related mobile alerts is also an option. Make it a priority to get as much work done without being interrupted. Interruptions make it difficult to get things done. It's not easy to get back into the work mindset if you take a break in the middle of a task. Try to finish what you're doing before moving on to anything else while you're working on a project. If you're trying to get something done, put everything else on hold.

You shouldn't, for instance, interrupt what you're doing because you remembered you needed to reply to an email midway through. Rather, jot it down in your to-do list and return to it once you've finished the current assignment.

Remember that interruptions are sometimes unavoidable. Try to keep your work environment free from distractions, but don't be too hard on yourself if you get interrupted occasionally.

Here are a few ways to better manage your time at work so that you can get things done.

   1. Get up early to extend your day.

   There are the same number of hours in each day for everyone. It's impossible to add more time to a day, but you may make your day go longer than average by getting up earlier. To function at peak efficiency, your body requires a minimum of six to eight hours of sleep every night.

You can start by waking up 15 minutes earlier than usual and gradually working your way up to a full hour earlier. This spare time can be put to good use by engaging in physical activity, mental reflection, the establishment of priorities, or the pursuit of a passion. You'll gradually become more productive each day, and time management won't be an issue for you again.

2. Instead of hoping for the best, plan for it by creating SMART objectives.

Goals should be S.M.A.R.T., which stands for "specific, measurable, attainable, realistic, and time-bound." Achieving these objectives will provide you with a firm foundation in your professional life and set you up for success in the present. We'll get into the SMART philosophy in more detail a bit later.

3. Find a suitable time-tracking program

Using a time-tracking program is a simple approach to monitoring how much time is spent on various tasks. These time management programs allow you to plan your work, monitor your progress, and see exactly how much time you've spent on each project.

4. Find your comfort zone

You've probably observed that there are some times of the day when you have laser-like focus and a surge of energy that allows you to get a lot done. It occurs when mental states match those of the surrounding environment. Others call it getting into "the zone," but the term "flow" is more common.

Discovering your "flow" or "zone" is a key factor in making the most of your time. Your zone is the time of the day you're most productive. You can achieve a peak level of awareness in which you are at your mental and physical best with its aid.

5. Avoid interruptions by closing off access

Some of the most regular and significant interruptions at work come in the form of emails, phone calls, and social media posts. Actually, you're losing a lot of hours daily due to interruptions at work. For this reason, it takes more than three hours to complete a task that normally would take only 60 minutes.

If you want to get serious work done without interruptions, you need to put your phone in silent mode and switch off data. You might increase your productivity by getting work done faster when you manage time correctly.

6. Focus on quality, not quantity

If you take satisfaction in the fact that you can perform a large number of chores at the same time, I have some news for you. According to the findings of a study, just 2% of individuals have the ability to multitask well. Multitasking is counterproductive and a waste of time for the other 98% of the population.

It's better to concentrate on one item at a time and really take it in than to divide your attention between many different things. The use of time limits has been shown to increase productivity. Allocating a certain amount of time to complete each work improves the odds that it will be finished on time.

7. You should take breaks, recharge, and refocus when necessary.

Despite appearances, taking breaks when necessary is a productive method of time management. Managing your time effectively doesn't always require choosing between two options. It also stresses the value of taking short breaks every hour or so to boost productivity because the more tired you are, the less productive.

8. Look for inspirational materials, such as books, films, or quotes

Sticking to a routine or following a set of rules might get old. When your internal motivation is low, it might be difficult to focus on your task. Put your time to better use by finding ways to motivate yourself rather than squandering it.

Stick some of those inspirational sayings about time management on your workstation. Watch videos on inspiration or TEDx, or listen to audiobooks, to pick up some pointers on how to better manage your time at work.

9. Stop procrastinating now

We're all too acquainted with the procrastination phenomenon, in which people postpone and delay getting tasks done. Those who are habitual procrastinators get a peculiar high from putting off pertinent tasks until later and then thrive on the anxiety of not having enough time to complete their tasks. You shouldn't make procrastination a habit that controls your life.

Separating your task into smaller, more manageable chunks is an effective strategy for beating procrastination. It not only makes it practicable but also offers you a starting place to begin work. Make sure you have a thorough timetable to provide you with a clear picture of when things need to be completed.

10. Get 7 to 8 hours of sleep each night

Sleep deprivation is a major problem that has both beneficial and harmful effects on society. Sleeping for six to eight hours a night not only helps you feel refreshed and revitalized, but it also supports your efforts to live a healthy life. Diseases including obstructive sleep apnea, obesity, and more are made more likely when adequate sleep is not achieved.

When the body and brain are well-rested, the result is improved judgment and efficiency. You are able to make a snap decision on what to do, when, and how to accomplish it. Create a routine for your sleeping hours and adhere to it religiously. Sleep and wake up at the same hour each day.

11. Outsource or delegate

Just as you would in the office, you don't have to do it all when it comes to organizing any facet of your life. Delegating and outsourcing tasks can greatly lessen your workload and free you up to focus on what really matters. Learning to delegate work and letting others help carry the weight is a sensible move no matter where you are in your career.

Outsourcing or hiring a freelancer is an option if you find it challenging to delegate responsibilities or allocate time for training others. Delegating tasks and bringing in outside help may be huge time saves if done properly.

I recommend trying out each of these tools to manage distractions one by one to see which ones best fit your lifestyle. It will be impossible to block everything out so you can focus strictly on your specific goals, but it is possible to try out a few of these techniques to see if they can help you organize your focus so you can organize your life!

CHAPTER 5: MONITOR YOUR PROGRESS

"We often overestimate how often we do things, but tracking eliminates this weakness. When we track we just have the facts, not our subjective reflections."

– Betsy Ramser Jaime

No matter how big or modest your goals are, tracking your path to success is crucial. The knowledge of what is and is not effective is a powerful tool. You need to be able to devote additional hours to actions that move you closer to your objectives. This is why you must know fully well what is and is not helpful for your newly-organized lifestyle. Eventually, you can identify and eliminate non-productive activities from your life. So, how do you monitor your progress and how do you measure it?

First, complete a weekly review to see how far you've come, where you can improve, and how important tasks are.

What you focus on expands into reality. It's been proven that the more you dwell on or discuss an event, the more likely it is to materialize. In order to function at your best, it is important to ask yourself the following introspective questions:

- So far, what have you found to be successful?
- What is your takeaway from the process of working towards your goals?
- Where do you see the future going, and what kind of expectations do you have for it?

Don't spend time worrying about the worst-case scenario when you reflect on how this process is coming. Instead, think about all you have done well. Also, consider your options for the future. Then be humble when sharing your success with others.

The next step is to keep a notebook in which you can record your thoughts and observations to evaluate your development. This might bring you a pleasant impression that will help you achieve future success. At the end of a week, I ask myself, "What did I learn? To what extent have my abilities developed? Where do I want to focus my efforts next week?" It's important to stop every so often and assess how things are going. Perhaps once every 14 days, give yourself some time to contemplate, either alone or with another person, the following topics:

I wish I could say this whole process is simple, but it's not. You're not just rearranging your house and taking out the trash– you're rearranging your way of thinking about organization, and taking the time to really think about what you need in your home, office, and life!

SECTION 3: ORGANIZE YOUR HOME

Be brave, and ask yourself these questions:

- *Does your house have a lot of mess and clutter, or is it clean and organized?*
- *Do you hang on to items that you no longer need?*
- *How clean is your garage? Or is it simply an extra place to throw your trash and unwanted items?*
- *Do your surroundings resemble the environment you desire?*
- *Is your home where you feel drained, or is it where you feel most inspired?*

It's difficult to move forward when you're surrounded by disarray and have no idea where to start. However, according to experienced organizers, the path to change isn't actually that nerve-racking, first, go inwards, then design a strategy to address those concerns.

When you have guests around, which room do you feel the most self-conscious about showing to those who are visiting your home for the first time? Which room in your house most often conjures up images of mayhem, disarray, or overload for you?

To begin, I always want to know, "What stresses you out the most?" And with that, we'll get started with how to organize your home.

CHAPTER 1: DECLUTTERING

"Simplicity Boils Down To Two Things: Identify The Essential, And Eliminate The Rest"

– Leo Babauta

Getting your life in order and clearing away unnecessary items may make your daily routine more manageable. Most of the time, disorganization is not to blame for a chaotic household that requires excessive time and effort to maintain. The underlying reason behind this is an excessive amount of stuff in your house, to begin with. There's just too much clutter!

Keeping an excessive number of belongings that you do not use, require, or enjoy can lead to clutter. Clutter and excessive time spent managing possessions are problems that no amount of organizing can fix. You can only find a long-term solution to your clutter if you deal with the reasons behind it.

By learning a few simple ways to get rid of clutter, you can stop your house from looking like a mess with little effort, making it feel like the peaceful place you've always wanted it to be.

How to Declutter in 3 Steps

Step 1: Remove all items from the room.

Knowing what you have in each area is essential for decluttering and organizing your room. This process even involves emptying the cupboards! After removing everything from its hiding place, deciding what to keep and what to file away will be less of a chore.

Make sure to clean the area thoroughly once you've moved everything out. Sweep the floor, clean the carpets, and wipe down the shelves. If you need to clean a large area or a particularly messy part of your home, you might want to divide it into smaller sections.

Step 2: Categorize what's left as "stay" or "go."

After you've chosen what you don't want to get rid of, sort through what remains to determine which objects belong in the room again and which ones may be better kept in another part of the house. Immediately after completing the space, relocate any items that will be stored elsewhere to their proper locations. Don't let things pile up in a new location and become extra work to organize.

Step 3: Declutter with aggressiveness

To successfully clear your space of clutter, be honest with yourself and master the art of letting go. You should examine each possession and decide if you really need it, want it, or cherish it. Would you purchase it now if you saw it in a store? Do you feel that it improves your life in any way? If the question can't be answered with a "yes," then it's time to let it go.

Don't forget to keep a trash bag and a storage basket handy to help you organize anything you wish to get rid of or give away. Decluttering for the first time in a long time isn't easy, but it's worth it when you consider the benefits: a calmer, more pleasant space; less time spent cleaning and searching, and more time spent enjoying the things you cherish.

Tips for Decluttering

Hold on because this list is a doozy. However, each of these tips can provide you with direction in getting your home organization troubles under control!

1. **You should first clean and clear any flat surfaces you have.**

Remove everything from your counters, tables, nightstands, and other flat surfaces for an instant decluttering effect. Spread everything out on the floor and put back just the necessities. Next, sort the remaining items into drawers, containers, or hangers. The change will blow your mind!

2. **Utilize storage areas that are underutilized.**

When living in a cramped apartment, having space under the bed is a godsend. By using soft bags instead of rigid containers, you can easily "overfill and squash" them under the bed.

3. **Determine which of your possessions you truly use and get rid of the rest.**

Purging items you know you won't use is the most significant part of any organizing process. It's only worth it to tackle a messy room or closet if you know, with absolute certainty, the items you want to keep.

4. **Designate a place for the clutter.**

All the stuff I bring into my house but haven't found a place for yet or intend to utilize in the future goes on a little shelf in my closet. On this shelf, you'll also find items that have yet to find a permanent place. It's important to designate a space for junk to prevent clutter from spreading throughout the home.

5. **Have a "one in, one out" policy.**

Having fewer things in one's house is the easiest organization technique I've come across. We can do this by instituting a policy whereby no item may be purchased unless an old one is donated or replaced. Alternatively, you may make an effort to be pickier about what you let into your house. This not only makes it simpler for you to maintain order in your home, but it also helps you save both money and time.

6. Put all of your belongings in their proper places.

It'll be much less of a hassle to return things to their proper homes if you've designated a specific location for each item. Returning items to their "home" helps prevent clutter build-up of things you'll deal with "later."

7. Make a decluttering checklist.

When you can see where you are in relation to your goals, it's much simpler to maintain focus. Make it a weekly ritual to clear up the top spots where clutter tends to accumulate in your home.

8. Pick and choose what you'll keep.

You should do a closet audit and get rid of anything that you haven't worn in over a year. Determine whether or not an item is worth keeping. You may have a hard time trying to decide whether or not to retain something because of the memories associated with it. Give yourself one large, transparent plastic bucket to pack your treasures in, and donate anything that no longer has meaning or use for you

9. You may help others by donating your unused stuff.

Become an advocate for a charity that assists others that are less fortunate. Knowing that your unwanted possessions will be donated to a worthy cause might make parting with them less of a chore. By donating your unwanted items, you are helping organizations create safe spaces for women, help victims of domestic abuse, and support nonprofit organizations.

10. Try Minimalism.

Minimalism simply means "less is more." Having less but the most important items. When trying to clear the clutter from my house, I've found that having less stuff works best. Items can be sold for profit or donated to charity, depending on their condition and value. Consequently, you'll have fewer possessions, and you'll have an easier time maintaining and arranging the ones you do have.

11. Create a system for keeping things.

When you're done sorting, you'll have a clearer picture of your available closet space. The best way to handle your possessions is to plan ahead. For example, keeping frequently used items where even the kids can easily get them will help reduce the frequency and severity of their messes.

12. Start a timer for 30 minutes.

Pace yourself so you can stay focused and not burn out. You can do any amount of cleaning at a time if you find that 30 minutes is too much work. Breaking down a huge task into smaller chunks of dedicated time can make the whole thing easier to handle.

13. Seek another opinion.

To be sure you don't miss anything, have a friend or family member over to assist you in searching the house for more opportunities for tidiness. Perhaps they can help you determine which items are worth keeping and which are better left behind.

14. Set smaller, more manageable goals.

Stop trying to clean your house in one sitting! Feeling overwhelmed is natural, and it's probable that you'll give up before you finish. Create more manageable objectives, such as clearing out one drawer on a Saturday afternoon or deciding to give away five articles of clothing.

15. No more multitasking for you!

When you decide you want to declutter a space, create a specific objective and deadline and stick to it. Don't let the many things that could distract you while you're decluttering stop you from doing what you set out to do.

16. When you put something out of sight, you're less likely to think about it.

Mark a box "maybe" for things you're still on the fence about keeping. Whenever you are on the fence about whether or not to keep anything, whether it be clothing or a piece of furniture, put it in the box and forget about it for a while. Examine it again at a later time to see if there are any items you may part with.

17. Make a central landing zone close to the entrance.

One way to reduce the accumulation of everyday clutter is to have a specific spot in your home where you can drop your keys, handbag, sunglasses, etc. as soon as you enter. Not only will it be less of a hassle to find your keys, but you'll be able to do it more quickly, too!

18. Avoid having too many duplicate items by sorting your closet by color and clothing category.

It's not enough to simply hang all of your shirts in one section of your wardrobe; you also need to sort them by sleeve length. Next, sort your clothes by color within each sleeve length category. It will be easy to determine whether you have too many of an item and pick which ones to donate.

19. Verticalize it!

It is recommended to use hanging racks wherever possible. It will be easier to get to the things you use most often, and it will aid in keeping flat surfaces clear, which is essential for a clutter-free environment.

20. Make a shamble of things before you try to order them.

To begin efficiently organizing and streamlining your possessions, you may first need to create an even bigger mess. If you want to give this method of decluttering a try, you should start by removing everything from its storage location, whether that's removing all of the food from your pantry shelves and piling it on the floor or removing all of the t-shirts from your dresser drawers and piling them on the floor. After that, you can give each item a full once-over and find a new place for it, all while keeping the shelves and drawers clutter-free.

Decluttering is not without its benefits. Among the many benefits of decluttering are:

- You can quickly locate items and maintain an inventory.
- Spend less time and energy on keeping your house neat without sacrificing cleanliness.
- Put together a house that is both beautiful and practical.
- Keep the quantity of stuff you own under control

Better yet, after you've done a thorough job of decluttering, organizing will be a breeze. When there is less to organize, doing so is easier and less of a chore. It's simple to find homes for the things that matter to you after you've made a place for them in your house.

CHAPTER 2: HOW TO ORGANIZE YOUR KITCHEN

Kitchens are the focal point of many homes because of their central location. Given the amount of time spent preparing, eating, and socializing over food, this seems like a good place to begin.

Tip 1: Declutter

Start the organizing process with a thorough edit. Empty the cupboards and drawers. Then get rid of duplicates and throw away anything that has expired. Get rid of anything that's taking up too much room in your cupboards and drawers. If it's an item that you actually use but doesn't fit in your space, consider donating that one and buying one that will neatly fit in your storage space.

Tip 2: Lay Out Your Space

To make the most of your resources, you must first catalog them. It's important to maintain some flexibility in your planning: Before you start rearranging things in the kitchen, make a plan on how you want things to be stored. This way, you can save both time and energy by following the plan. The cooking tools (spoons, spatulas, flippers, tongs, etc.) should be separated from the rest of the utensils and placed in a drawer close to the stove. whatever tools you use to prepare food (such as can openers, juicers, garlic presses, and so on) should be stored in a drawer beneath your prep area.

Tip 3: Utilize Drawer Dividers to Straighten Out the Clutter

I think drawer dividers are some of the most underutilized tools on the planet! Do you want to keep things organized in your storage drawers? These are attractive and quite useful, perfect for storing and displaying anything from dishcloths to cooking implements. Again, in my opinion, they are the most important tools for arranging kitchen drawers.

Tip 4: Rearrange Your Kitchen Cabinet

Remember that the shelves within your cabinets are adjustable. Raise or lower the shelf so that you can reach things easily. You can also make more room so that things aren't piled up in unsafe ways. Most frequently used things should be stored on lower, more accessible shelves. Also, don't pile too much stuff onto the shelves. I recommend giving yourself enough room to reach for things and then stow them away.

Tip 5: Combine Several Forms Of Storage

You'll likely need a variety of kitchen storage options to keep things in order. So put non-perishables in containers and use baskets for perishables like breakfast foods and snacks. Organizing your kitchen will benefit you greatly. It will result in: Easier meal prep, less kitchen waste, more time for enjoying meals with your family or friends, and lower take out expenses.

CHAPTER 3: HOW TO ORGANIZE YOUR LIVING ROOM

Every house has a living room that serves as the hub of family life. So keeping it organized can be difficult, but extremely important when trying to keep a tidy house. The good news though is maintaining its order is a breeze; just follow these few steps.

Step 1: Make Room On Your Coffee Table

The coffee table is a focal point of any living space, so avoid keeping unnecessary objects there, find another place for the clutter on the table.

Step 2: Always Put the Remotes Back Where They Belong

There are few things more annoying than sitting down in front of the TV, only to realize you can't find the remote. Create a haven, if you may, for your remote, and keep it there!

Step 3: Put Away Soiled Dishes

Is there a mountain of dirty dishes in your family room? Get them to their rightful places! Develop a habit of keeping dishes in the kitchen immediately after eating.

Step 4: Fluff Your Pillows And Fold Your Blankets

Just a minute before hitting the hay, commit to this nightly ritual: Fluff the throw pillows and replace them on the sofa; then, fold the blankets. And ta-da! A well-organized room you shall have!

These may sound like silly, simple things, but here's the secret: once you've fluffed the pillows, you'll probably start looking for more opportunities to tidy up your living space. You might realize that things are piling up where they don't need to be. Do the simple and easiest chores first so you can be inspired to continue taking more steps towards organization.

CHAPTER 4: HOW TO ORGANIZE YOUR BEDROOM

Your bedroom is the last thing you see when you go to sleep at night and the first thing you see when you wake up in the morning. You want to make sure it stays in pristine condition. Your bedroom should be inviting and relaxing, making it the perfect place to actually rest.

Step 1: Get Rid Of The Clutter On Your Counters And Tables

Get rid of the clutter on the main furniture in your space – from dressers to desks and nightstands. Keep the number of things on your dresser, nightstand, and other flat surfaces to a minimum. Getting rid of the unnecessary items in your bedroom will help make it a more relaxing and restful space with fewer distractions when falling asleep, and less anxiety when getting ready in the morning.

Step 2: Make Your Bed

Every morning, make your bed. This quick fix will have a dramatic effect on the way things look! The bed is the largest flat surface in your room, keeping it arranged and free of clutter will easily make your room look more organized.

For many of us, our bedroom is our haven— a place to recharge and rest. If the state of your bedroom makes you feel anxious, you are probably not getting the rest you need. Depending on how cluttered your bedroom is, you may need to go piece by piece to determine what needs to be thrown away, donated, washed, or put back in its original place.

As you do this, think about patterns you see in your mess. How can you implement an organization method that helps you prevent clutter from taking over? Perhaps you get hampers for clothing in various stages of use- clean, mostly clean, and dirty. What if you added a trash can beside your bed? Make use of drawers, storage bins, and closets so you can find everything you want without any stress and go to bed without a mess looming over you.

CHAPTER 5: HOW TO ORGANIZE YOUR CLOSET

It's not going to be fun getting ready for the day if your drawers are overflowing and clothes are scattered all over the floor. Having a relaxing place to sleep at night and get ready in the morning can have a profound effect on how you approach the day.

Step 1: Sort Your Wardrobe

Take a good look at your closet, purge the items you seldom wear, and sort the rest into useful categories. One method for keeping track of one's wardrobe is to divide it into sections (tops, dresses, skirts, etc.). You'll have an easier time getting dressed and a better idea of what you have in your closet if you do this.

Step 2: Streamlining Your Hangers

One of the most noticeable changes you can make to your wardrobe is to use uniform hangers. It instantly makes your wardrobe look more streamlined and refined. Make sure all of your garments are hanging in the same way once you've acquired a sufficient number of matching hangers. Also, ensure the top button is closed on button-ups and that everything is hung so that the same side is facing out. This helps to maintain a minimal aesthetic and can help you throw on the perfect outfit with no stress at all!

Step 3: Fold And File Away In Drawers

One approach to keeping your drawers neat is to "file fold" your items, which involves flipping each folded item on its side so that the edge of the fold is visible. You may save a ton of room by keeping your shirts and smaller items file folded in drawers. As a bonus, you'll be able to easily select the right garment for your perfect outfit.

It's easy to let our closets become a place where more mess can hide, but maximizing your closet space for organization means you can find everything easily. You may wish to pull everything out of your closet and ask yourself why you're letting it pile up and hide. Does it need to be thrown away or donated? We often put things in a closet so we can deal with them later, but maybe today is the day you deal with them!

CHAPTER 6: HOW TO ORGANIZE YOUR BATHROOM

Bathrooms see a lot of wear and tear! However, the good news is that their size makes them quite easy to clean and organize. Here is a procedure to follow to keep your bathroom looking great, no matter what you throw at it!

Step 1: Buy Lots of Stackable Bins

The bathroom storage system you choose can help you maintain order. Furthermore, a great way to maximize your storage area is to stock up on stackable storage bins. To make the most of the area beneath the sink, use a variety of different-sized stackable containers. Similarly, you can make use of the vertical space offered by bathroom cabinets by installing stacking drawers. You can maximize organization in these bins by sorting similar items together. For example, hair products in one, toothbrushing and oral hygiene equipment in another, makeup, skincare, etc.

Step 2: Make Use Of Drawer Dividers

Many bathrooms have multiple chests of drawers. Therefore, it is reasonable to acquire some drawer dividers, as they'll help compartmentalize everything.

What about towels and linens in the bathroom area? Keeping the sink/toilet/bathing area clean? What types of cleaning and maintenance equipment belong in the bathroom? (plunger, toilet brush, etc)

As you take a look around your bathroom, how clean do you feel it is? If giving your bathroom a good scrubbing hasn't been important, you may wish to keep your cleaning supplies within easy reach. This can mean in a cabinet or linen closet, or on a shelf if space is limited. This may not force you to clean your bathroom regularly, but it will make it easier for you to clean when you have all the tools you need in sight.

CHAPTER 7: KEEPING YOUR LAUNDRY AREA TIDY

Don't forget about the laundry room when you're decluttering your house; it's easy to forget about a place that you rarely go into.

Step 1: Don't Let Laundry Linger

The first rule for having a tidy laundry area is to always put clean clothes back where they belong. Don't leave clean laundry lying around; fold and put it away from the place where you got it. Then make that part of your routine every time you're done with laundry in order to harness the force of habit. With piles of clean laundry waiting to be folded, a laundry room may quickly become disorganized.

Step 2: Spruce Up Your Space with Containers

Second, use containers to neatly store your equipment. Investing in attractive containers to keep your laundry supplies organized is a simple but effective way to boost the aesthetics and effectiveness of your laundry room.

Sometimes, people find that it's easier to start with one area of the house. You can start with your bedroom, and after focusing on it for a few weeks or months, broaden your organization to other rooms of your home. Others prefer to start with consistently performing one task across the whole house, such as always picking up dishes. Then they add more tasks, like picking up dishes AND always using hangers for their clothes. The choice is yours, but being consistent is important!

CHAPTER 8: HOW TO KEEP YOUR HOME ORGANIZED FOR THE LONG TERM

Imagine doing all of this and in a week, everything is back to square zero. That would be frustrating, to say the least! That means you'll have to consistently maintain your home's newfound order. It's recommended that you do a few of the more manageable tasks on this list every day, or at the very least once a week. For example, every day, before leaving the house, you should make your bed, and every night, you should return your dirty dishes to the kitchen and put away your clean laundry.

Maintaining order is a lot like keeping a clean house; the initial effort is always there, but if you've set up a decent system, it's much easier to keep it that way. And try not to lose heart if things go wrong. This could be used as a confirmation bias on your part to further the false belief that you are disorganized.

Instead of giving up hope, set new objectives and make new plans until the project is finished. Don't forget to honor your achievements, either. As humans, we tend to be in a constant state of motion, never pausing to acknowledge our accomplishments before moving on to the next task. You should celebrate your successes. When things go wrong, don't despair. Take the time to refine your objectives and give yourself a new shot at success.

A Call To Action: Start Organizing Your Home Today!

- Clean your immediate surroundings.
- Get rid of anything and everyone in your life that doesn't make you happy.
- Try investing in bins or containers that can make the organization process of the home easier and more attainable/ long-lasting.
- Maintain a focus on vitality and simplicity by keeping only the things you need.

SECTION 4: ORGANIZING OUTSIDE THE BOX

For many of us, "organization" means "getting rid of the mess." But, as you saw in the last section, there's more to it than that. Organization means prioritizing, arranging, and giving your attention to things in order so that it makes sense and causes the least stress.

That means there are some areas of your life where you can apply the same decluttering techniques you used on your physical space. Chances are good that if your house is messy, you are struggling with organization in other areas of your life, too.

It's time to dig deep and inspect your life to see what other areas could use some tidying up!

CHAPTER 1: ORGANIZE YOUR MIND

"Set peace of mind as your highest goal, and organize your life around it."

— Brian Tracy

If you're like most people, you have about 70,000 thoughts per day, and if you don't learn to corral them, they can seriously disrupt your life and work. Chaos in the mind happens when you give in to the constant stream of thoughts, and focusing on unpleasant and unimportant thoughts only makes them stronger.

The vast majority of our assumptions are really just that—assumptions, not facts. It's not easy to halt the forward motion of your thoughts when you give credence to the negative, distracting, and gloomy things your inner voice says. Research shows that mental disorganization is detrimental to your health. High levels of stress, persistent negativity, and impulsive behavior are the results of a chaotic mind. These problems make it hard to get things done and are linked to a number of diseases and conditions, like obesity, heart disease, insomnia, and migraines.

Conversely, a well-organized mind enters a state of flow. When you're in the zone, you're completely absorbed in what you're doing and your mind doesn't wander. The ability to reach a state of flow allows you to do your best job while also enjoying it. When people are in a flow state while working, they are more productive than when they are not in that state.

You might find that following these three guidelines will help you to get your day off to a good start and stay on track throughout the day:

1. Regulate Your Feelings

You have to get control of your bad emotions before you can concentrate on anything. The prefrontal cortex becomes impaired and overwhelmed by this chaos, making it impossible to "think straight."

You can't think clearly or stay healthy if you're constantly operating under the weight of stress. The good news is that boosting your health also bolsters your mind's capacity to calm anxious thoughts. Get enough sleep, work out, practice mindfulness, or just take it easy every once in a while. Find your own method for controlling your anxiety and maximizing your concentration.

2. Just Get It All Out of Your Head

Get it out? Get what out? Absolutely everything... as well as actions, thoughts, worries, questions, and ideas. Get it all out! Don't bother with organizing them just yet. Just let them go so they can stop circling and taking up valuable mental resources. Next, examine the tasks you have pending and consider whether or not you want to attend to each one today.

If that's the case, add the tasks to your to-do list. But if you don't want to take any steps today, put them in a journal, paper, or idea file to revisit later. Write down any current worries so you can think about them logically when your mind is settled. The beautiful thing is, if they aren't that significant, you'll forget to revisit them later.

3. Try Not to Let Your Attention Wander

Specify a single activity that must be completed. Introduce your brain to the purpose of the concentrating session, which is increased productivity. To begin, try closing the door, turning off your electronic devices, and setting a timer for twenty to thirty minutes. When put into practice, these "laws of order" will alter not only your focus patterns but also your outlook on life. You won't be anxious, but rather coolly in charge.

As a result of your increased productivity, you will be able to devote more time to activities that are good for your physical and mental well-being. Feeling good about oneself is beneficial to one's physical and mental well-being. And your newly-found mental order will serve you well while you work toward your health and fitness objectives.

CHAPTER 2: ORGANIZE YOUR MONEY (AND BECOME WEALTHY)

Have you accumulated any unneeded debt? How much money do you spend each month? Do you make as much money as you'd like? These are tough questions to answer, right?

You see, few people keep track of their spending. If they did, the money they spend on things like eating out would probably be shocking. It wasn't until I made money management a top priority that I was able to achieve financial success. Put simply, if you want anything to happen in your life, you need to make your finances a priority. The question then becomes how to set financial goals.

The process of setting financial goals is clear. First, you set really specific and lofty monetary objectives and you justify your efforts to reach your objectives with compelling WHY statements. You commit to learning the ropes of personal finance through books, mentors, and the hard-won experience of others.

Also, you need to start putting money into yourself and your own personal/professional development, your plans for the future, either through retirement savings or other investment vehicles, and your most important connections; if you're not putting effort into them, they're not going to improve.

Gaining even a modicum of order in your finances will allow you to launch toward a prosperous financial future. So, now is a great time to take stock of your financial life and make any necessary adjustments to ensure that your efforts are paying off, whether you're saving up for a special occasion like a vacation or just want to feel more secure with your money in general.

Like tackling a cluttered attic, facing your financial situation can be daunting, especially if it's something you've been putting off. Budgeting, savings objectives, and insurance policies may seem overwhelming, but there are easy solutions to clean up these three areas of your financial life. If you follow the guidelines below, you'll be able to get your money in order and develop a management strategy that works for you.

Step 1: Create A Budget And Stick To It

The first step in getting your finances in order is to gain a thorough understanding of your present financial standing. Creating a budget is a good way to focus your efforts. Many people indeed associate the word "budget" with negativity, but that's not the case. Having a budget does not restrict your options. It gives you the freedom to do more of what you want to do.

Learn the source and destination of your cash flow by keeping a record of your receipts and expenses. Check out the many helpful and often free budgeting and money-tracking applications in the Organizing Tools chapter. Numerous apps now offer integration with various payment systems, allowing you to easily keep track of your purchases, payments, and deposits by linking to your bank account or credit card. Follow these guidelines to make a sensible financial plan:

Step 2: Create a Long-Term Plan

The most popular rule of thumb is the 50/30/20 rule: 50% of your net income goes to needs, 30% goes to wants, and 20% goes to savings, investments, or debt reduction. Choose a plan that works for you and stick to it; the best budget is the one you use.

Step 3: Choose a Budgeting Tool

Don't try to do it alone. It might be time-consuming to keep track of all the money coming and going. You should instead utilize a budgeting tool, a simple spreadsheet, or cash envelopes to keep track of your monthly allocations and spending.

Step 4: Track the Budget and Actuals

Simply noting your planned expenditures is not sufficient. Keeping track of your monthly expenditures is a requirement. Next month's spending plan should be based on this data. If you manage to save money, you can put that money toward other goals. If you go over budget, you may have to cut back on something else.

Step 5: Find a Reliable Accountability Partner

If you can, have a friend or family member check in on your budgeting efforts every so often. Automating your financial transactions, such as bill payments and savings, is another good method of maintaining your routine.

If you're having trouble fitting your debt payments into your budget, try prioritizing the repayment of individual debts. You may build your self-assurance and keep the momentum going by tackling the smallest debt first.

Bear in mind that your financial condition is dynamic, thus your budgeting approach should be flexible. As you reach milestones, pay down debt and increase your income so it will continue to evolve. At the very least, take stock of your progress toward your objectives and revise your spending plan accordingly each year.

CHAPTER 3: PLAN A SAVINGS STRATEGY

With a healthy savings account, you can secure your financial future and take care of any immediate expenses. Any savings strategy for retirement, an emergency fund, or investments like a mortgage, stocks, or mutual funds, should be based on the tenets of SMART goals. SMART goals are:

Specific: The definition is crystal clear and there is no room for ambiguity.
Measurable: With quantifiable metrics, your success in achieving the objective can be tracked in real time.
Attainable: You can accomplish your goals in a reasonable amount of time.
Realistic: Accessible, doable, and meaningful to your life's mission; these are the hallmarks of a realistic goal.

Timely: having a specific beginning date and ending date for the undertaking. Urgency is intended to be created.

If you want to save $20,000 in the next two years for a down payment on investment property, you will need to put away around $834 every month. You can factor this sum into your budget so that you know where to put any windfalls in terms of savings or income. If you keep focused, you might even attain your goal much faster than expected.

Select Suitable Resources

Maintaining a regular savings routine is challenging without the proper resources, such as bank accounts and payroll deductions. Having savings contributions automatically deducted and direct-deposited from your paycheck might be useful. You can earn rewards for saving and protect your purchasing power by opening several types of savings and investment accounts, such as those that pay interest, those that don't charge fees, mutual funds, etc.

Check Your Current Insurance Plan

While insurance is important for safeguarding possessions, few individuals check in on their policies to see if they still provide adequate protection. It's a good idea to examine your insurance coverage every spring. First, it's important to review the original terms and make any necessary changes to the policy's beneficiaries to make it more relevant to your present situation.

It's easy to let budgeting, objectives, and coverage slip your mind when life becomes hectic, but doing so can lead to greater financial clarity and peace of mind now and in the future.

A Call To Action: Organizing Your Finances

- Make lofty plans for your savings and stick to them.
- Choose to achieve financial independence.
- Be sure to keep a record of your money.
- Think carefully about where your money will go and where it shouldn't.
- Put up a sizable amount for retirement (for instance 10% of your salary).
- Put significant time and money into developing yourself, your connections, and your business. Start giving money away to causes you care about.
- Build trust with your accountant and get your tax situation under control if it isn't.
- Hire a financial planner or develop a strategy to start saving for the future.

CHAPTER 4: ORGANIZE YOUR RELATIONSHIPS

Do you find the most happiness and fulfillment in your interactions with other people? Do you put in enough effort to maintain your most important relationships? Do you keep people in your life who are no longer beneficial to you? Do you treat others genuinely and with honesty?

Most people's social lives are as chaotic as their financial ones. A love companion deserves our full attention and careful consideration. But as the excitement of a new romance wears off, we tend to slack off. We begin to forget that first spark, and we stop investing time and resources in it. The immense possibilities our relationship once held no longer excite us. As a result, we start to act carelessly. When we stop making memories, the magic stops happening.

As we quit following our own set of guidelines, we begin to converge with the norm. Our relationships will suffer if we do this. A religious leader, Thomas Monson said, "Choose your love, then love your choice," which is a beautiful saying. Search for the one who makes you feel drawn to them. To develop a great relationship and vision with that individual, you should do everything in your power to serve them. Then, continue to put effort into bringing that person happiness and building a stronger, more expansive vision.

Make sure your most important connections don't become jumbled. keep your partner in your thoughts, and know what they enjoy. Determine the specific steps you'll take this week to strengthen and invest in your relationship. Keep your focus on the end goal, which is a happy and satisfying relationship, and let that drive your actions, thoughts, and level of contribution to others. It's undoubtedly breaking apart if you haven't given it any thought in a while.

5 Tips To Better Organize your Relationships

How well do you handle your dates and relationships? I've put together five pointers to help you maintain your edge (and out of trouble).

#1. Mark Your Calendar: As frustrating as it is to have a date you failed to keep, there is nothing worse than having multiple. Stop making excuses for your forgetfulness and start scheduling your meetings in advance on your phone using the calendar feature. The next step is to schedule a reminder.

#2. Add Color Coding To Your Address Book: Do you have several dates lined up with different people? It's embarrassing to send a text to the wrong person, as everyone who has done so knows. Contacts can be color-coded to make messages stand out.

#3. Plan Ahead: Even though impromptu or surprise dates can be fun, the best way to stay on top of everything is to plan. Having a flexible schedule will provide room for these joyful experiences, but a packed agenda might quickly overwhelm your personal life.

#4. Cut Off Loose Ends: Time is of the essence. If a particular platform or person isn't working for you in your dating life, you shouldn't devote time and energy to it.

#5. Access your Progress: Effective dating habits lead to a more streamlined social life. The fruits of your labor in the dating world will become apparent if you commit to regularly assessing your progress.

A Call To Action: Decluttering Your Relationships

- Consider your top 10 relationships and write them down.
- Put down on paper the reasons you value these connections.
- Where do you think these connections currently stand?
- Do you intend to shoulder all of the load in terms of how well you work together and how this partnership develops?
- In what ways have you worked to strengthen this connection over the previous week to a month?
- Determine your desired outcomes for this connection and work toward them.
- Do something special and unique for them that shows a lot of consideration.
- Maintaining these connections should be a major priority.
- Maintain the same level of effort you put into the connection whenever possible.

The last item in that list is particularly important, because what happens when you start putting effort into your relationships is remarkable. Wonderful and uncommon chances present themselves. Strong bonds between people form. Relationships are an investment, whether you build them casually, romantically, or professionally. Make magic happen in your relationships, rather than just consuming the benefits. Set some objectives for yourself. Act considerately and kindly toward others.

Five Steps You Can Take to Organize Your Social Life

The idea of planning one's social life is foreign to the vast majority of individuals. Business life organization, like file organization, makes sense, but why would you consciously organize your social life? Let the good times flow organically and unplanned– isn't that the point of having friends? Not entirely. Intentionally cultivating deep and meaningful relationships in order to socialize, make friends, and have fun is the goal. If you have a ton of free time and want to spend it socializing on the beach, you can make those dreams come true with organization and perseverance. However, if you're like the vast majority of individuals, you probably have a hectic schedule, and a lackluster social life is all too possible as a result. In this case, making an effort to arrange things consciously is necessary. Get your social life in order by following a few simple tips I've compiled for you.

Step 1: Prioritize Your Social Life

Things that don't seem urgent or a priority to us tend to garner less of our focus. In the same vein, social gatherings like parties and family picnics might feel like a chore. However, if you prioritize work relationships over personal ones, you will soon find yourself lonely and regretful. The first step is making up your mind that you will not put your social life on the back burner.

Step 2: Remember to Record Your Social Plans

Once you've decided that maintaining your social life is important, it's common sense to include it in your schedule. In conclusion, a calendar is a great tool for keeping track of both work and social commitments. In this way, you won't wind up missing that special birthday you meant to celebrate because you overbooked your schedule and forgot about the party.

Step 3: Understand the Value of Each Relationship

It's important to recognize that not every friendship or acquaintance is equally rewarding. Investing time is important if you desire a successful social life. However, this is not always easy to do, since we all have that one acquaintance who is perpetually wanting to hang out at the most inopportune times. To keep your social life in order, it's vital to learn to say "no" to some people so that you can devote more time to the relationships that matter.

Step 4: Group Folks Together and See What Happens

If you're constantly swamped with too many commitments to make time for socializing, bringing people together can be a good solution. As an alternative to meeting friends one by one, you could meet three of them at once, introduce them to each other, and have fun with all of them at the same time. While not as intimate as a one-on-one conversation, group discussions nonetheless have the potential to feel warm and friendly (especially when the proper people are included).

Step 5: Prioritize Frequency Over Length

Rather than interacting with someone for extended periods, meeting or interacting with them frequently is more effective in building and maintaining a relationship. Having coffee together once a week for 30 minutes can have a lot more significant psychological impact on your relationships than spending a week together once every six months. As much as possible, be mindful of this, and plan your social activities accordingly.

Eventually, by following each of these steps, I was able to turn my social life around from a chaotic disaster to one of the most rewarding aspects of my existence. Now I actively seek out opportunities to connect with new people, whether they be friends, acquaintances, or potential business partners virtually every day. When you invest your time, effort, and attention in your social life in a strategic manner, you come to appreciate how crucial interacting with friends may be to your well-being.

CHAPTER 5: ORGANIZE YOUR HEALTH AND FITNESS

Is there a purpose behind everything you eat? How does what you eat affect other aspects of your life?

How well does your physical form represent your ideal self? How strong and fit are you? When compared to how you felt three months ago, how much better off are you now? Are you working out more frequently and more intensely? What else is there to care about if not your health?

You will perform significantly below your full potential if you're not in perfect health. If you and your significant other are both healthy, but your relationship lacks spark, you should consider making some changes. Having a healthy body is of high value. It's easy to neglect our bodies by skipping sleep, relying too heavily on stimulants, and eating poorly.

It's the little things that add up, Eating poorly too often, Not working out enough. Everything runs together in the end. However, your health, and hence your confidence and mental acuity, will improve if you take care of it. You'll have greater drive and enthusiasm for everything you do.

Maintaining a healthy lifestyle may be accomplished through a more structured approach to daily life. Check your schedule, and try to incorporate some time for exercise during the next two weeks. If you put exercise on your schedule, you'll be less likely to cancel it.

When it comes to eating healthily, meal preparation that has been well thought out is more helpful rather than regularly consuming junk.

If you take the time to get your space in order, you'll find that it encourages you to get in a workout. It's easy to put off working out because you can't find your gym clothes, but if you lay them out the night before, you won't have that excuse.

A Call To Action: Be Honest About Your Health

- Do not ignore your health and take an honest look at it.
- Consider your health in the next twenty to thirty years; this will help you make wiser choices in the here and now.
- Decide on a plan to better your health.
- Motivate yourself to get into the best shape of your life by giving yourself a goal
- Keep your goal in mind at all times, and use it as a rallying cry whenever you feel the need to undermine yourself and your accomplishments.
- Avoid mindless snacking before bed.
- Get outside and walk more.
- Take in lots of fluids.
- Feel the adrenaline rush as your self-assurance grows.

Chapter 6: Organize Your Work Life

"Organization is not an option; it is a fundamental survival skill and distinct competitive advantage."

— Pam N. Woods

Time is money, and you may waste a lot of it if you are disorganized. The moments you've wasted dealing with disorganization add up to hours. But even if you do accomplish all of your daily tasks, your job performance may suffer. The extent to which you are able to stay on top of your work and meet deadlines has a significant impact on your professional success and, in turn, can have repercussions for your colleagues and team members. Calm and order are stress-busters and productivity boosters.

Why It's So Important

Most modern organizations have adopted the attitude that all employees should be proactive, professional, and show initiative; organization skills are one of the most sought-after talents in new hires. Taking responsibility for your work and proving that you don't require close supervision are both emphasized when you maintain a high level of organization. You see, a person's own actions are ultimately responsible for their level of organization. You can't rely on your supervisor or coworkers to keep you on task. Relationships at work could be jeopardized if you consistently need followup or reminders to do your job.

Maintaining organization in the office has positive effects on your team as a whole. For instance, when everyone uses the same file naming convention, everyone benefits from the system's efficiency (including you). Meetings are more effective when people show up on time.

The Positive Effects of Better Organization at Work

Productivity and efficiency gains are the primary advantages of working in a clean, uncluttered space. As a result, one experiences a greater sense of life control, which is essential for effective stress management as well as your overall health and wellness.

If you're well organized, you might even find that your ability to problem solve improves as a result. Having a level head and access to relevant data and resources is essential for decision-making and problem-resolution. Your focus and ability to learn will increase with fewer distractions, and you'll be well on your way to the "flow" state of intense concentration that comes from doing an activity with complete absorption.

Furthermore, your reputation at work is a major factor in your overall professional success. Consistently missing meetings, slacking off on tasks, and giving the impression that you can't handle your position all hurt your professional credibility and make advancement down the road less likely. But if you do a good job of setting priorities and contributing to the smooth running of your team or company, your value and skill will be clear.

The 3 Essentials of Office Organization

Don't forget to work on these three essentials to improve your general organizational abilities:

- Your office space
- Communication
- Time

Let's take a deeper look at these essential tips for staying organized at work.

1 Get Your Office In Order

Your desk (or primary work area) is a fantastic place to begin your organization process. Just how helpful is your existing work area in keeping you organized? If you find that everything is exactly where you need it to be to get your job done, don't try to change it. However, if you find that your messy desk is affecting your productivity, it's time to make some adjustments.

What do you need to have within easy reach? Look around and put things away. Throw them away if they aren't being used or are just taking up unnecessary space. Create a designated space on your desk that you can call your "action area," where you can put the materials you'll need for whatever you're working on at the moment. For instance, if you're currently working on compiling reports for your manager, consider having a notepad and pen handy to jot down notes. If the reports need to be printed, make sure you have a folder and stapler nearby so you don't have to spend time trying to find the tools you need to get the job done. As a result, you'll be able to get started on your work sooner, concentrate better, and finish in record time. When one job is done, make room for the next one by putting everything in its proper place.

Additionally, once you have created a neat and tidy office environment, do your best to keep it clean. . Make a decision on what you'll need every day. Put less important but still necessary objects in desk drawers or file folders. Anything you don't need can be given away to other office mates, or properly destroyed according to office policy.

2 Make A Plan For Communication

Clear communication is another benefit of good organizational skills. You'll have an easier time remembering and discussing ideas and facts if they are all in your notes, where you've meticulously structured ideas. With this information at hand, you can make your communication more useful, relevant, and perhaps even persuasive. In addition, you may have a reassuring sense of serenity and self-assurance.

This is particularly helpful when you need to act or respond rapidly, such as during a crisis. When you are able to communicate clearly, you'll have a clearer picture of what steps to take next. Also, you'll be able to respond with more poise and conviction.

Keeping your work environment free of distractions allows you to better manage your time and, in turn, perform at a higher level. You can get more done in less time and with less hassle if you make the effort to get your workspace, schedule, and communications organized.

3 Plan Your Schedule

The ability to manage one's time well is directly correlated to one's organizational skills and vice versa. Taking a less chaotic approach to your work can not only save you time, but will also help you make better use of the time you do have. In a similar vein, having access to adequate resources and data is necessary for efficient planning and scheduling. The time it takes to complete each task can be more easily estimated when you have quick access to all the resources you require. You'll also know exactly when to do each task so that it fits in with the rest of your work and upcoming deadlines. One of the most important aspects of effective time management is maintaining a level head throughout the day. Each day should begin with the same resolve you've had during the previous ones. Write down a list of things you need to get done, prioritizing what you can. You'll be able to better shape your day by prioritizing your schedule. You'll know which items are the highest priorities and which may wait till later in the day. You can also schedule your most important or difficult tasks for when you're at your peak productivity. Read on for an in-depth exploration of time management techniques.

SECTION 5: PRACTICE ACCOUNTABILITY

Self-accountability is a major part of the organization process because it helps you prioritize your objectives and get insight into your motivations for pursuing them. Now you might think "oh! It is just about organizing this and that part of my life and prioritizing, no need to stay accountable." Well, news flash, self-accountability is as essential in your home as it is in your office and everywhere else. Contrary to what you may believe, you have to stay accountable for your organizational process. Accountability strategies can help you feel more empowered to get things done.

Think about it for a minute; with accountability:

- The standard of your work can be assessed.
- You can lend a hand to those who are trying to make a difference with organizing. This may involve lending a hand to those in your immediate circles, such as coworkers, relatives, and neighbors.
- Your level of confidence is something you can work on. If you take the time to figure out the most efficient means of accomplishing your objectives and meeting your responsibilities, you could find that you carry yourself with more assurance throughout the day or in that place.
- Improving one's ability to self-manage and organize leads to increased insight into one's work, which in turn better equips one for future endeavors.

CHAPTER 1: 8 WAYS TO STAY ACCOUNTABLE AND ORGANIZED IN YOUR LIFE

Accountability and organization go hand-in-hand. When you decide the time has come to become organized, and you hold yourself accountable to that goal, you'll be more motivated to make organization a part of every aspect of your life.

1. Create a Long-Term Objective

Keep yourself accountable because you want to achieve your long-term objective. Here, the goal is broad: organizing your life!

2. Set Short-term Goals

Speed up your progress toward your long-term objective by setting weekly short-term targets. Set some goals for the week and pick which day you'll check in on your progress. Making goals that can be accomplished in a very short period and that are specific may be useful. If you want to get your life in order, one of your short-term goals could be to declutter your home.

3. Define Your Values

Think about the things that are important to you and what drives you to achieve. If you take the time to reflect on why you want to organize your life(home and work included), you may find that you are more motivated to do so and can come up with more effective methods of holding yourself accountable. If you want to give more attention to a specific value, try writing a few memorable, actionable sentences that will inspire you. You may wish to narrow or expand the scope of this statement at a later date or for a different activity.

4. Prepare A Schedule For Yourself

Create a timetable that will allow you to accomplish your short-term objectives while still meeting your other obligations. Think realistically about how much you can achieve in a given amount of time to stay on track and still get the work done. It could be useful to compile all of your tasks into a single timeline document. Here, you'll want to set priorities for not one, but two, near-term objectives: one that you're particularly excited about achieving, and another that both have tight deadlines at work or should be done urgently at home. Effective time management and reliable estimation are two abilities that might benefit from this kind of exercise.

Achieving success is easier if you know what to do and when to do it. And if you're having trouble finding the will to clean up your act, all you have to do is put your mind to it and take action. When you know how much you need to accomplish this week, you can plan accordingly. Second, schedule this for a day when you don't have a lot going on.

5. Count the Frequency, Not the Duration, of Each Action

Quality over quantity is a common adage. However, it doesn't hold in this situation. It is vital to keep track of the number of times you work on a goal rather than the goals themselves. Let's use the kitchen as an example: if you want to get it in order in two weeks, you should plan on doing a little bit every day. Instead of being disappointed that you didn't get more done at the end of the first week, you'll feel better knowing that you did something every day. Focus on doing bits of the work frequently, and you can stay accountable and on the right track.

6. Get An Accountability Partner

Some people have found having an accountability partner to be useful so you may want to consider getting one to help with your goals. Get a buddy, coworker, or acquaintance to discuss common accountability targets and decide on a schedule for regular check-ins. Generally, finding someone with the same long-term objective can help you provide more targeted input. You may help keep each other accountable and motivated all week long by trading accountability strategies and inspiration.

7. Design A Vision Board

A creative technique to keep yourself motivated on your chosen route is to create a visual representation of your long-term or short-term objectives. The purpose of a "vision board," is to create a central place where you can collect images and words that inspire you. If you have a passion for creative expression, this tactic may work best for you. To make a personal vision board, just choose a large piece of poster board or paper and decorate it with magazine cutouts, online articles, images of organized homes and offices, quotes about organizing better, and more.

8. Reward Yourself

For every part of the house or the office you organize, reward yourself. Creating a reward system naturally will help you remain accountable. How? You'd feel motivated to achieve more and you'll begin to notice when you don't do something you were meant to.

CHAPTER 2: MENTAL HEALTH, ACCOUNTABILITY, ORGANIZATION, AND YOU

Do you ever feel overwhelmed by the demands of daily life and wish your home and life were better organized? I know it's not simple to get everything to fit together, but there's a lot more to consider besides clearing the clutter if you want an orderly life and house.

I don't think you can feel completely in control of your house and life until you address all of these issues. Let's take a closer look at each one individually, and then you'll understand why it's important to view the broad picture, and why I want you to work through all these areas so you can get your home and life in order.

You might find it strange that I bring up mental health when discussing organization, but the truth is that if you don't take care of yourself mentally, you won't be in a good place to accomplish your goals of becoming more organized in your home and daily life. Your motivation and attitude toward routine chores will suffer if your mental health is not stable.

If you take care of yourself emotionally, physically, and mentally, it will show in your interactions with others and your work. The first step toward getting yourself in order is to tune into your emotions and prioritize your mental wellness. You can't get through your to-do list efficiently if your head isn't in the game. Your performance time on tasks increases. It's counterproductive to put off doing the simple things you have to do every day because you don't feel like doing them.

Getting organized takes less time and energy when there is less stuff to sort through. Because you don't have as much stuff, you don't need as elaborate a system for keeping it all in order and neat. One of the easiest and quickest methods to make a better-functioning, more organized home is to clear the clutter and get rid of anything you don't use, need, or enjoy. Always start by clearing the clutter from your home. Reduce the amount of stuff you have to organize by getting rid of the things you don't use or need. Furthermore, you will avoid the trap of accumulating more junk. Starting with a clean slate will help you save time, effort, space, and money as you begin organizing. Less clutter means you need fewer (or no) storage solutions like baskets and containers. You won't squander cash arranging things you no longer want, need, or desire to keep!

As a final piece of advice, make sure to keep up with the routines you've put in place to keep your home organized and functioning efficiently. Even the most well-planned and well-designed home organizing system will fail if you don't put in the time and effort to keep it that way. The good news is that it shouldn't be that challenging to keep them if you create straightforward, well-thought-out organizational structures.

SECTION 6: ORGANIZING TOOLS

If you're like me and you're always looking for ways to streamline and improve your efficiency, organizing tools are a great way to do both. Organizing tools could be an application or software that would help simplify the process of getting better organized.

Sadly, the constant interruptions from our mobile devices simply serve to add stress to our already tight schedules. It's up to you to decide whether or not you want to let your phone complicate your life. These tools and programs will serve you well in many ways, including time tracking, habit formation, reminders, and more. They make your phone an extremely efficient tool.

While the ideal app may vary from person to person depending on specific requirements, the following selections should cover most bases.

Permit me to point out that you shouldn't try to implement too many of these tools at once, and you definitely shouldn't spend too much time testing out each one of them individually. Choose your favorite(s) and run with them. You can always try something different if they don't work, but it's more essential to pay attention to the action itself than to the tools used to carry it out.

Finances

When our financial situation is chaotic, it can make us feel as if we have no control over our life. It's not as daunting as it seems to take the time to create a budget and keep it. Get your financial house in order with the help of some excellent resources.

You Need a Budget (YNAB): If you want to keep track of your spending and see how it compares to your budget in real-time, YNAB is the perfect program for you since it syncs across all of your devices and provides you with practical guidance as you create a sensible spending plan.

Mint: Another safe program that might help you keep track of your finances is called Mint. Spending can be broken down into categories, account balances can be synchronized, and all of your data can be viewed in one convenient location. The user may select a financial plan, establish objectives, and track their progress from their computer or mobile device.

Time

The importance of time management cannot be overemphasized. Using the applications below might help you use your time more productively.

Toggl: Toggl is a time management program that helps you keep tabs on your productivity. Toggl is a Chrome plugin that places a timer on top of any website or web app, allowing you to keep track of how much time you spend using each one. It simplifies planning and prioritizing your activities for the day. In addition, it has sophisticated capabilities like idle detection for tracking when you're most and least productive throughout the day. Time spent in each app can be monitored. Discover when in the day you are at your peak productivity. Plan your day so that you can get the most done in your most productive hour.

Smarter Time: Smarter Time's mission is to help you get insight into your time usage so that you can better plan your day. It is even capable of automatically tracking your activity: The software will try to fill in the gaps in your day based on your past patterns and information gathered by the phone's sensors, even if you're supposed to just be keeping track of your time.

Once you begin entering information into this software, it will generate reports detailing your daily activities, including which programs are hogging the most of your time. Then, if you want to alter your day-to-day activity ratio, you may create unique targets that Smarter Time will assist you in achieving.

Pocket: It's easy to become lost in the depths of the Internet, and many of us do just that. You don't have to read an article right away, even if you find one that piques your curiosity. Do yourself a favor and save it in Pocket to read later when you have more free time.

Pocket is a bookmarking service that works with mobile and desktop browsers, as well as with Gmail, Facebook, and Twitter to save articles for later reading. To facilitate future retrieval, you may assign tags to the articles and videos you've saved. If you've already saved a few articles to Pocket, the app will begin suggesting others you might enjoy
.
You may read offline with this app. The articles you save to Pocket will be stored in a cache for later reading. Additionally, it will synchronize your collection across all of your devices if you install it on more than one.

Clockify: Clockify is a time management tool that helps you ease into each day. Easily visualize your workweek and stay on top of your calendar with the Calendar view of this all-in-one organizing and time management solution. This program may also be used to visually analyze the workweek, organize and plan tasks, and track time from anywhere online.

Planner

Microsoft Planner: With Microsoft Planner, you can easily create and use boards for planning. You may categorize work for each strategy on its own board. Tasks can be organized in several ways, including by status and by the assignee. Keeping track of all of your tasks is easy.

One of the most useful features in Microsoft's Office 365 suite is Planner. All you have to do is make some tasks, set due dates, add some people to the team, and include some comments. It keeps everything out in the open and in plain sight, and it syncs with your workplace and calendar so that notifications appear automatically.

DayViewer: DayViewer is a user-friendly online planner that consolidates calendaring, note-taking, task management, and other similar functions into a single, accessible location, regardless of the device being used. It's a tool for organizing your time and projects that will boost your efficiency. Logging your daily activities is simple with the journal app, and staying organized is a walk in the park using the label management system.

To-do list management is simplified with the use of push notifications on DayViewer. As a bonus, it's also useful as a digital notepad.

Akiflow: By supporting users in avoiding the most common errors that have a negative impact on productivity, Akiflow enables multitaskers to accomplish more in their workday and remain on top of their game. Like having a personal assistant, Akiflow is a helpful online planner that both groups and individuals can use to coordinate their efforts and stay on top of their plans and projects. Using Akiflow, you may stay focused and productive without having to deal with the negative effects of multitasking, interruptions, or constantly moving between different tasks. To help you remain on top of your organization, Akiflow employs a set of clever keyboard shortcuts.

Google Calendar App: Using the Google Calendar app, you can save time that would have been spent organizing your day and use it for what's really important: doing things!. In order to guarantee that you are maximizing the use of your time, you may schedule activities and chores in advance on your calendar.

Coolendar: Some of us prefer a list style for our daily schedules, and that's exactly what you get with this calendar app. Using Twitter, Instagram, and other social media sites, you may sync with pals and share plans using personalized tags. For even more efficient task management, you may set up several reminders in other apps, such as email and Twitter.

SpotOn.it: Whether you're organizing a seminar for your company, a charity gala, or a ticketed event, you can use the interactive calendar at SpotOn.it to keep track of all the details. You may use it to keep track of upcoming events or to include calendar entries on your own website. To your convenience, the app can scan the pages you browse for upcoming events and add them directly to your Google calendar. You may also use it to keep track of local sporting events, concerts, and other activities.

File Sharing and Storage

It is possible to save data and transfer it between your computer, smartphone, and tablet with the aid of one of various "cloud" sharing tools. There is often a free tier of storage with many of these programs, with paid tiers offering greater features.

Dropbox: Keeping things in order isn't simply restricted to planning events, chores, and projects. How you keep your files is just as essential as how you keep everything else organized, and programs like Dropbox make it simple. You may access your data, photos, documents, movies, and more from any computer with the help of Dropbox. Because of Dropbox's intuitive interface, you no longer need to send yourself attachments via email. Dropbox is a cloud storage and file-sharing service that allows its users to easily back up their data and share files with anybody else who also has an account.

Cloud Storage from Google: Drive, like the rest of Google's services, allows you to synchronize your data across all of your Google products, such as Gmail, Blogger, Picasa, and more. Drive is a file storage and sharing service that supports a wide variety of file types and allows for simple reading and editing.

Google's Keep: The first step is to choose a good note-taking tool where you can place all of your random notes, checklists, and ideas. Google Keep's user-friendliness and cross-platform availability make it a favorite of mine.

Google Keep does a lot more than just save your notes; it also provides a number of options for structuring them. You may easily organize anything that has to do with "home," "work," "the kids," and so on by labeling connected items in a similar color or tagging them with certain terms, for instance. This makes it possible to color-coordinate relevant entries. You have the option of storing a number of different types of notes, including texts, lists, doodles written with your fingertip or a stylus pen, voice recordings, and photos.

Notes made in Google Keep may be shared with other users, or converted from plain text to a Google Docs file for a more polished presentation.

To-Do Lists

I like making lists and I find them useful for many purposes. It's a wonderful tool for organizing information visually. You may assign things numbers and mark them off as you do them, set due dates and due periods, and even assign each task a different color. Paper lists are used by some, whereas computerized ones are preferred by others.

Google Tasks: Google Tasks is a "to-do list" tool that is straightforward, excellent, and user-friendly. It is accessible from your inbox or calendar, and you may even access it on your mobile device. Time limits, reminders, and deadlines may be set up for tasks, and the lists can be checked off as they are finished. If you like using paper lists, here is a simple alternative to consider!

Notebooks: We're all aware of paper notebooks, but this online software does a similar job without the possibility of getting lost in the mayhem. You may convert any note to a to-do list with the use of Notebooks' Dropbox synchronization features. Notebook is a basic software that can be used the same way as your favorite notebook, including writing notes and keeping track of to-do lists.

Todoist: There are several useful list-making applications if you prefer not to write lists by hand. Todoist is among the most popular task management applications out there. This all-encompassing utility supports a wide variety of systems, comes with a clean and simple UI, and allows access to more complicated options for those that want them.

This program, for instance, allows you to prioritize your tasks. It's possible to create hierarchies of tasks and use layering to keep personal and professional lives distinct. If you need to remember to do something every week, like putting out the trash or paying your phone bill, you can establish a recurring task in Todoist so that it will remind you at the appropriate time.

Sunsama: Sunsama is an excellent online organizer and software, whether you need something to keep track of chores or a versatile tool for making daily or weekly to-do lists. Countless reputable businesses have put their faith in Sunsama, including Spotify, Uber and Hubspot, etc. Using Sunsama, professionals who juggle several responsibilities may complete critical work in a timely manner and better organize their schedules. Sunsama is compatible with both Outlook and Google. Every day, you should check in on the progress your team has made and see what they have been up to that day.

Reminders

Sticking a note on anything might serve as a handy reminder every now and again whether that's a digital note, or a very tangible piece of paper.

Post-its: Of course, the old classic is Post-its, and they are a simple method to provide a reminder to oneself, family, and friends.

Sticky Notes App: Sticky notes are meant to help you prioritize your day's work by separating your to-dos into three categories: "Must Do," "Should Do," and "Would Like to Do," so that you can "eat that frog" and accomplish the most essential task. It also pushes you to think ahead about how you'll reward yourself for a job well done and helps you see the day's accomplishments before you even begin.

Squareleaf: Squareleaf improves upon traditional sticky notes by allowing users to organize their notes on a "virtual whiteboard." This application is a lot of fun and a terrific planning tool for those of us who are very visual and enjoy rearranging things. It's particularly useful for dynamic planning, for when you know you'll have to make a lot of adjustments as the project develops. When you require a lot of leeway, this is a great alternative to consider.

Project Management

Whether you're a blogger, a company owner, or just need a way to coordinate the efforts of several people on a single project, a straightforward project management tool may be invaluable. Many of them are too "robust" for typical household requirements, although they may be easily adapted for mundane tasks.

ClickUp: As a terrific organizing tool and a straightforward platform for managing projects, ClickUp is hard to beat. With its intuitive interface, users can quickly switch between multiple project views, which are organized in a hierarchical structure. The process of coordinating and overseeing group initiatives is simplified as a result.

Asana: Asana is yet another excellent company with powerful project management features. The intuitive design of Asana's interface facilitates group and individual projects alike. Its timeline function is useful for visualizing project timelines and establishing task interdependence.

Asana is a project management app that allows users to coordinate their efforts on a common board. It provides a continuous snapshot of the whole process and the current production levels of all participants. Collaborative file sharing, email and calendar synchronization, and task management are all possible features.

Evernote: It's easy to share files and keep track of project notes using Evernote. Aside from being powerful enough to handle photos and bigger files, it also allows you to carry your notes with you while you're not connected to the internet. Internet articles may be "clipped" and saved as digital snapshots for later use. Individuals who want to "storyboard" their endeavors before plunging in will find this to be an invaluable tool.

Get Plan: Get Plan serves as a personal assistant in the office. Smartly integrating with your email, GitHub, JIRA, Salesforce, and Zendesk, Salesforce. It streamlines your team's workflow and makes it easier to stay on top of all your projects. As a result, you'll have more time to devote to actually performing the task, rather than spending it figuring out how to accomplish it. A centralized destination for all of your apps. Build a plan, categorize your tasks, and monitor your advancement. Make sure your team has its own separate area to operate in.

Organizing Software

There is an abundance of high-quality software available today that may be utilized for a variety of purposes, including but not limited to clipping coupons, creating shopping lists, arranging one's house, providing child care, etc. The list of excellent applications I could recommend would go on for pages, but I think it's preferable to focus on just a handful, to begin with.

Nuance: You may get this nifty dictation tool either as an application or as software. Having access to a dictation program like this is invaluable. Nuance will automatically convert your voice into text. It may replace your regular keyboard for taking notes, sending SMS, and writing blog articles for effortless use without the need for hands-on manipulation.

Habit List: The motto of Habit List is "Build a better you," and the app's features are all designed to assist users in accomplishing this goal. The program offers subtle prompts in the hopes that you'll adopt more desirable behaviors, including keeping on top of your documentation and maintaining a regular cleaning schedule.

The app's functionality consists of little more than marking off completed tasks on a calendar or setting up periodic reminders for new habits. The app will then provide you with progress updates to evaluate how well your new routine is working and prompt you to finish any outstanding activities. The easy nature of the daily to-do list that is presented to you upon waking up is only one example of how the uncomplicated nature of the interface contributes to your increased ability to concentrate.

Feedly: Like the newspaper headlines you see each morning, Feedly displays the stories and posts in short snippets. In a short amount of time, you may get a feel for the whole thing and dive into the things that interest and apply to you the most, giving you peace of mind that you haven't missed a bit.

Trello: Although Trello is best known as a collaborative tool for teams, it may also be used by individuals or families to organize their own tasks or those they work on together. This is due to the fact that Trello's adaptability makes it suitable for a wide range of uses.

Both the smartphone and online apps for this service function in the same way, allowing you to make digital "cards" and arrange them in columns. An upcoming event, a duty around the house, or a to-do list item might all be represented by a different card. The columns may be used to include types of work, levels of urgency, due dates, or anything else that helps you organize your cards.

After settling on a system for categorizing your cards, you may give each one more specific information to make them more manageable. Include a brief explanation, some color coding, the names of anybody who should get notifications or reminders, and a due date on the card. After that, team members may interact with the cards by writing notes, uploading files, and rearranging their positions. Any level of complexity in your Trello arrangement is entirely up to you.

24me: 24me is another great software for staying on top of your busy schedule. It helps you keep track of your ideas and your day by providing tools like a to-do list, calendar, reminders for chores and events, and note writing. It's easy to make notes and schedule meetings with the help of the voice control feature. The ability to take notes by just speaking is a unique capability offered by voice control. Intelligent alerts to help you keep track of your schedule and not forget anything. Also, it is compatible with a wide range of scheduling apps.

Home

One thing I would advise against doing if you're trying to get your house in order is to keep buying additional bins to store all your things, as the true problem is generally too much stuff, not a lack of containers. However, there are a select few devices that I have found to be indispensable in the process of decluttering and organizing.

Label Maker: I can't stress enough how beneficial it is to identify everything. Labels make it obvious that assigning a specific location for each item is essential to achieving and maintaining order.

Any.do: Keeping your life in order is not just a skill useful in the workplace. Keeping in mind to finish a project report is similar to remembering to deliver a birthday card to a buddy. The greatest organizational applications streamline every aspect of your life's orderliness. In a nutshell, Any.do is a life-management app that streamlines the process of organizing everything. Creating and overseeing a number of separate projects in a snap. Your smartwatch may also be used to access this. Helps you keep on top of things by letting you make a plan of action.

Kids Stuff

Parents understand that children naturally have an enormous quantity of clutter. It's impossible to free yourself of this clutter permanently, despite your best efforts to declutter. I have found the following objects helpful for keeping kids' belongings organized:

Bookshelf With a View of the Front: Kids have a hard time keeping their books organized in traditional bookcases. A straightforward, front-facing book storage system that makes it simple for youngsters to find what they need is the obvious solution.

A Basic Toy Chest with a Lid: Even though a wall of perfectly labeled containers could make things look more ordered, in actuality, most children won't keep them that way. Having a single, lockable toy box that youngsters can toss their toys back into is a convenient option. Toys that are no longer being used should be rotated out or discarded.

Wall Locker: Having a convenient spot to put coats, shoes, and backpacks is an important but sometimes overlooked part of keeping kids' belongings tidy and organized. Kids will appreciate having a secure area to keep their belongings in this basic wall locker, and you'll appreciate not having to clean up the books, dirty shoes, and homework tracked around the home!

When decluttering your home, you wouldn't use a box that wasn't the right size, shape, or condition. Apply the same method while selecting tools to help you organize in your home or workplace. Do not use them unless you have confirmed that they will indeed help accomplish your desired results. Discovering and putting into practice what works best is the best method for achieving success.

When faced with too many possibilities, it's helpful to remember the "simplicity principle" and focus on using only one or two tools to their maximum potential.

CONCLUSION

Hi! Welcome to the end and the beginning. It's the end because I have to say goodbye, and it is the beginning because the real work begins when you close this book. We have talked about everything from the basics of organization and why you should get organized to the importance of prioritizing and how to automate. So, let me just reemphasize some points.

People who are consistently well-organized have likely done the hard work of developing those habits over time. That being said, if you consider yourself a highly disorganized person, know that you can acquire the skill of organization. If you are prepared to put in the time and effort, you can learn to become more organized in all aspects of your life, from making plans and keeping lists to getting rid of clutter and focusing on what really matters. Getting your life in order is the first step toward achieving fulfillment. Keeping yourself organized is a simple way to remain on top of things and keep stress at bay. Getting your life in order is a learned skill that improves with regular practice. When learning how to get your life in order, it's important to approach things slowly and methodically so you don't feel overwhelmed and give up.

So take down notes. Everyone has that one friend or family member that always recalls special occasions and makes an effort to reach out with greeting cards. They don't rely on memorizing or magic to do it. Keeping a journal may help. A pen and paper are our external, more lasting means of remembering information. If you try to keep all of your reminders and schedules in your head, you will simply make things more chaotic for yourself. Make note of everything!

The time of the well-organized is never wasted. They understand that remaining productive is inextricably linked to maintaining order. Planners create and maintain daily and weekly itineraries. They establish objectives and timelines. The most essential part is to follow them! If your life is disorganized, you won't be able to meet your deadlines or accomplish what you set out to do. Think of creating a bucket list as an experiment. Make a list of everything you want to accomplish this year and in your life. Then, establish a plan of action to get there. Make the most of the time you have by focusing on the things that are truly important to you.

Never Put Things Off! It will be more challenging to complete an undertaking if you wait too long to start working on it. Get your life in order as soon as possible if you want to reduce the amount of pressure and chaos in it. If you make an attempt to complete tasks as soon as possible, you'll have less to do afterward. Consider just one aspect of your life that could benefit from some sort of order as an exercise. Put it in writing. The next step is to document the time frame in which you can complete the task and the resources you will require. Go ahead and do it now if you can!

Moreso, you may want to find a place for everything. If you don't have a fixed location, it's easy to become disoriented. Having everything in its designated spot is essential for maintaining order. Properly storing items and clearly identifying storage areas are two ways that organized people maintain order. Don't let your storage areas become a dumping ground for random items; instead, designate specific areas for goods you use frequently. Find innovative solutions for storing your belongings. As an exercise, try rearranging just one room in your house. In the event that things are dispersed, put items together. When you're done sorting, put things together in a home you discover or construct, and then label the homes and put the goods inside. Put things you use frequently within easy reach, such as a cup holder for your pens and pencils, while stowing away the stuff you don't use very often.

Set aside some time every week to get your life in order. A highly organized person schedules time once a week, if not more often, to sort through and put away their belongings. Things don't stay in order by themselves; they require constant and regular reorganization. Try looking at your schedule and finding a time to organize, and then actually do it.

Don't hoard; only keep the essentials. More possessions equal more mess. Those who maintain a tidy home and life only keep the items they use or truly desire. If you have fewer possessions, you're more likely to make use of them all rather than letting half of them gather dust.

To see if your expectations match reality, try making a list of all the items you believe you need. Then, make an inventory of your possessions. It's time to get organized if the quantity of your possessions has grown to the point that it conflicts with your list of essentials.

In the same line of thought, don't forget to get rid of as much as you can. Give to charity shops. Use online marketplaces like Craigslist and eBay to sell your items. Visit a local recycling facility. Throw a yard sale. Look for a dump or dumpster where you can dump your stuff. Just do something! Try decluttering just one room to see what happens. Search the cabinets, drawers, and storage bins. Put whatever you find that is unnecessary in a separate pile. Separate items between those you might want to preserve and review later and those you can get rid of right now. Then, figure out how to swiftly send those items packing.

Finally, do your best. When it counts, put forth the extra effort. The first step in organizing what has to be done and when is to assign tasks and create a schedule.

Organizing is not always simple. You'll need to put in some serious effort, but you'll be rewarded with a clutter-free home, an organized office, and well-managed emotions in the end. If today is the day you feel like giving up, double your efforts! Remember that your life having meaning for you is more crucial than all of the noise telling you what you can't accomplish.

Printed in Great Britain
by Amazon